The Secrets of Startup Fundraising
How to Raise Millions for Your Business

Table of Contents

Introduction

The Journey Ahead

Welcome, fellow trailblazers.

If you're reading this, I can only assume that, like me, you've embarked on one of the most challenging and rewarding journeys any individual can undertake – founding a startup. Ah, that wonderful whirlwind of late nights, brainstorming sessions, caffeine overloads, and those small victories that keep us going. It's a wild ride, isn't it?

I remember the early days of my startup, when it was just an idea scribbled on a napkin. But as the saying goes, "A journey of a thousand miles begins with a single step." That napkin was my first step. The road ahead was filled with obstacles, challenges, and some spectacular views, metaphorically speaking. But throughout it all, one of the biggest mountains to climb was fundraising.

Ah, fundraising. The word itself can bring forth a myriad of emotions. Excitement, anxiety, hope, fear—you name it. It's the fuel for our dreams, the lifeline that can propel our scribbles into reality. But like every treasured thing in life, it doesn't come easy. In fact, it's one of the most intricate dances we founders have to learn.

But why this book? And why from me? Well, just like you, I've been through the trenches. I've faced the piercing questions of sharp-eyed investors, the elation of a successful pitch, and the desolation of one that didn't quite hit the mark. I've seen the peaks and valleys of the fundraising landscape, and I'm here to share the map I wish I had when I started.

Imagine, for a moment, that we're sitting across from each other at a cozy coffee shop. The aroma of freshly brewed coffee fills the air as the soft hum of conversations create a comforting backdrop. As we sip our drinks, I lean in and say, "I've been there. Let me guide you." This book is that conversation. It's our heart-to-heart, where I share my insights, mistakes, victories, and those little secrets that can make all the difference.

In the chapters to come, we'll unravel the intricacies of fundraising, from understanding its basics to navigating the global investment landscape. You'll hear stories from my journey and lessons I've learned along the way. We'll laugh, we might shed a tear or two, but most importantly, we'll learn together.

So, dear founder, as we embark on this enlightening journey, I want you to know that while the path ahead may be challenging, it's also filled with incredible opportunities. With every page you turn, I hope to arm you with the knowledge and inspiration to make your dreams a reality.

Here's to the journey ahead. Let's dive in.

Why This Book?

Imagine this: A dimly lit office on a crisp autumn evening, filled with stacks of papers, half-empty coffee mugs, and scribbled notes capturing the essence of my entrepreneurial journey. At times, it felt overwhelming, and yet, the fiery spark to innovate and change the world never waned. In that reflective moment, a profound realization washed over me — how many others out there are braving this same storm?

Throughout this thrilling expedition of entrepreneurship, books have been my compass. They've whispered wisdom, shared tales of triumph, and offered comfort during the stormier nights. But amidst all the literary guides, there seemed to be a missing voice. The voice of a companion who truly understood the emotional and practical rollercoaster of creating a startup.

That void inspired the genesis of this very book.

Every hiccup, every celebration, every late night, and every early morning in my journey held a lesson, a nugget of wisdom. Some came easy, while others were learned the hard way, through missteps and stumbles. But every single one of those experiences crafted a lesson, valuable not just for me, but for every founder who dreams big.

So, why this book? It's my way of passing on everything I've learned. Every mistake I've made, every success I've tasted, I've distilled into these pages as my way of giving back. Because, at its core, entrepreneurship isn't just about business — it's about community, understanding, and shared growth.

To all the founders, the visionaries, the dreamers who dare to think differently, this book is my gift to you. It's a beacon, shedding light on the challenges, the joys, and the unparalleled journey of bringing an idea to life.

Together, let's traverse this path, embracing every lesson, every challenge, and every triumph. Because in this shared experience, in this mutual understanding, we find the true spirit of entrepreneurship. Let's dive deep, learn, and grow, turning our visions into realities.

2. **Understanding the Basics**

The Lifecycle of a Startup

The life of a startup. Ah, what a journey it is! If startups were living, breathing beings, their lifecycles would be among the most captivating tales nature has to offer. Every stage, every turn, brings its own set of joys and challenges. It's akin to watching a sapling grow into a mighty oak, facing storms and sunshine alike.

When I first began my own startup journey, I'll admit, I was a bit naive. I imagined it as a straightforward path—come up with an idea, get some money, build the product, and voila, success! But soon, reality painted a much richer, more complex picture. Each phase of the startup lifecycle had its own flavor, its own trials and tribulations, and its own unique beauty.

In the very beginning, there's the **Idea Phase**. It starts with a spark, a 'eureka' moment, if you will. Maybe it hits you during a morning shower, or while you're out on a run, or perhaps during a casual chat with a friend over coffee. It's that initial realization that there's a gap in the market, a problem waiting to be solved, and you might just have the solution. This stage is filled with excitement, doodles on napkins, and endless possibilities.

But then, the rubber meets the road. The **Planning Phase**. It's time to take that spark and craft it into a coherent business plan. What will the product look like? Who are the target customers? How will you reach them? These questions might seem daunting, but trust me, they're crucial. It's like drawing up the architectural plans before building a house.

Once the plan is in place, we enter the tumultuous yet thrilling **Execution Phase**. This is where things truly get real. Hiring a team, building a prototype, facing technical challenges, tweaking the product based on feedback – it's a whirlwind. And amidst it all, there's the hunt for funding, which is an adventure in itself. But through the chaos, there's also unparalleled joy, especially when you see your vision slowly turning into a tangible reality.

Now, if things go well (and I'm rooting for you), your startup blossoms into the **Growth Phase**. The user base expands, revenues climb, and there's a sense of momentum. The tiny sapling is now a young tree, reaching for the skies.

However, it's also during this phase that many startups face existential questions. How to scale? How to manage a growing team? How to evolve the product to cater to a larger audience? It's a period of introspection, strategy, and sometimes, pivoting.

Lastly, if all the stars align, comes the **Maturity Phase**. Your startup is now an established player, a force to be reckoned with. But with maturity also comes responsibility—towards stakeholders, employees, and the community at large.

Reflecting upon my journey, I cherish each of these stages. The giddy excitement of the initial idea, the grind of the execution, the satisfaction of growth, and the wisdom of maturity. Each phase shaped me, taught me, and most importantly, reminded me why I embarked on this path in the first place.

As fellow founders, I encourage you to embrace each stage of your startup's lifecycle. Savor the highs, learn from the lows, and remember, it's the journey that truly matters. As we move forward, I'll share more insights, lessons, and stories from each of these stages, hoping to guide and inspire you in your unique journey. Onward and upward, my friends!

What is Fundraising?

If I were to distill the startup journey into a blend of emotions, it'd be an intoxicating mix of passion, anxiety, exhilaration, and hope. And right at the heart of this cocktail is something that often remains a bit of an enigma: fundraising.

Ah, fundraising. The word itself evokes a myriad of emotions. I remember the first time someone mentioned it to me, my mind immediately went to charity drives and school events. But in the startup world? It's a whole different ballgame.

At its core, fundraising is about belief. It's about convincing others to believe in your vision, your team, and your drive. It's about translating your passion into a language that potential investors can understand – and that language, my fellow founders, is often spoken in numbers, projections, and valuations.

But let's strip away the jargon and the boardroom presentations for a moment. Imagine you're setting out on an epic journey across uncharted lands. You have the map, the vision, and the determination, but you need supplies and allies. That's where fundraising comes in. It's about gathering the resources you need and rallying people to your cause. It's about ensuring you have enough fuel in your tank and wind in your sails to navigate the inevitable challenges ahead.

Now, I won't sugarcoat it. Fundraising can be tough. I've had my fair share of doors closed in my face and investors who just didn't 'get it'. But I've also experienced the indescribable joy of someone looking me in the eyes and saying, "I believe in you. Let's do this." That moment, when someone else sees the potential in your dream and is willing to back it with their hard-earned money? It's nothing short of magic.

But it's also a responsibility. Because with their belief comes a commitment on your part to do everything in your power to make that dream a reality. It's a partnership, a pact that you'll navigate the highs and lows together.

Fundraising isn't just about money. It's about forging relationships. It's about understanding the market, knowing your worth, and communicating your vision with clarity and conviction. It's about finding the right partners who share your enthusiasm and can offer more than just capital – be it advice, connections, or mentorship.

As we delve deeper into this topic, I'll share stories from the frontlines – the pitches that floored, the ones that flopped, and the lessons learned along the way. We'll demystify the world of VCs, angel investors, and term sheets, making them a little less intimidating.

To my fellow founders, I say this: fundraising is both an art and a science. It's a dance of numbers and narratives. And while it may seem daunting now, with the right perspective and preparation, it can be one of the most rewarding parts of your startup journey. So, strap in and let's embark on this fascinating voyage together, unraveling the world of startup fundraising, one story at a time.

Key Terms to Know

Before we plunge deep into the world of fundraising, let's make sure we're speaking the same language. I remember my early days, sitting in investor meetings, nodding along, but occasionally getting tripped up by some of the jargon. Trust me, it's a bit like learning a new language. But, just like any language, once you get the hang of it, it becomes second nature.

Let's dive into some key terms that'll be your north stars as you navigate this exciting realm. And don't worry, I've got your back. We'll decode these together:

- **Equity:** This is ownership in your company. When you hear of startups offering equity to investors, they're giving up a piece of the ownership pie. Think of your company as a delicious pie, and every slice represents a part of the ownership. The more slices you give away, the less pie you have for yourself. But, remember, sometimes a smaller slice of a gigantic pie can be worth more than a whole pie of a smaller size.

- **Valuation:** Essentially, this is what your company is deemed to be worth. It's a blend of art, science, and a dash of optimism. Remember, valuation isn't just about numbers. It's a reflection of your potential, your team's capability, and the market's appetite. And, much like the stock market, it can go up or down based on numerous factors.

- **Venture Capital (VC):** These are the folks who manage pooled funds from many investors to invest in startups. They're not just looking for a return on their investment; they're often looking for a significant return, given the high risk associated with startups. Teaming up with the right VC can be game-changing. They bring capital, sure, but they also often bring a wealth of experience and connections.

- **Angel Investors:** Think of these as the guardian angels of the startup world. They're individuals who provide capital, often in the early stages, in exchange for equity or debt. Many of them have been through the startup grind themselves and are looking to give back, guide the next generation, and, of course, make some money along the way.

- **Term Sheet:** If fundraising is a dance, the term sheet is the music. It's a document that outlines the terms and conditions of your investment. It's not legally binding but serves as a blueprint for more official, legal documents down the line. It's crucial to understand every note in this symphony to ensure you're dancing to the right tune.

- **Burn Rate:** This one's pretty straightforward but oh-so-crucial. It's the rate at which your company is spending money vs. bringing it in. Keeping an eye on your burn rate ensures you don't run out of fuel before reaching your destination.

- **Exit Strategy:** This is your game plan for allowing investors to cash out and realize their return. Whether it's through acquisition, a merger, or going public with an IPO, it's essential to have an endgame in mind.

Now, I know this might feel like a lot to digest. I remember feeling a mix of excitement and nervousness when I first encountered these terms. But here's the silver lining: the more familiar you become with this vocabulary, the more empowered you'll feel in negotiations and discussions.

So, let's keep these terms in our back pocket as we forge ahead. With every chapter, with every story, they'll become clearer, and soon, you'll be using them as fluently as your native tongue. Ready to dive deeper? Let's go, trailblazers!

3. **Preparation: Laying the Groundwork**

Evaluating Your Business Model

Starting a new venture is a lot like setting sail on vast, uncharted waters. Sure, you have a map and a general direction, but the seas are unpredictable. And when it comes to navigating these waters, there's one thing that stands out for me as a founder: scalability.

Now, I've been around the block a few times, and if there's one consistent piece of wisdom that rings true, it's that investors are magnetically drawn to businesses that demonstrate scalability, even before they hit profitability. You might wonder, "Why is that?" The startup ecosystem thrives on rapid growth, on ventures that can take the momentum of today and turn it into a roaring crescendo tomorrow. This isn't your granddad's brick-and-mortar shop; in the startup world, if you're growing at a regular pace, you're likely falling behind.

Think about it. A traditional enterprise might aim for consistent, year-on-year growth. But for startups? The mantra is often 'go big or go home'. We're talking about week-on-week growth, pushing boundaries, and relentlessly innovating. It's a thrilling, sometimes dizzying pace, and it demands a business model that's built not just for stability, but for explosive growth.

So, when you sit down to evaluate your business model, it's essential to look beyond the basics. Sure, having a solid product-market fit is crucial. Understanding your target audience, having a strong value proposition, and knowing your competitive landscape are all foundational. But the million-dollar question is: How quickly can you scale?

In my own journey, I've found that scalability often hinges on a few factors. Flexibility, for one, is paramount. The ability to adapt to changing landscapes, to pivot when necessary, and to mold your business in response to feedback and market dynamics is a game-changer. Then there's innovation – not just in terms of your product but in how you deliver it, market it, and support it.

And, of course, there's the team. A scalable business model isn't just about strategies and market analysis; it's about having a team that's driven, agile, and aligned with your vision. A team that can take on challenges head-on, think on their feet, and drive that week-on-week growth that sets startups apart from traditional enterprises.

Evaluating your business model in the context of scalability is akin to ensuring your ship is not only seaworthy but also built for speed, agility, and the occasional storm. As founders, it's our job to ensure we're not just floating, but sailing with intent and direction.

To all my fellow founders, remember: in this fast-paced world of startups, scaling isn't just a goal; it's the very essence of the game. Embrace it, plan for it, and let it guide your every decision. Because when you're built to scale, even the vast, uncharted waters seem a little less daunting.

Building a Strong Team

Every founder's journey begins with a spark, an idea that promises to disrupt the status quo. But as any seasoned entrepreneur will tell you, while ideas might be the genesis, it's the team behind them that truly determines their destiny. Dive deep into the world of startups, and you'll quickly discover an unspoken truth: investors, more often than not, put their money on the team, not just the idea.

Reflecting on my own rollercoaster ride as a founder, I've come to deeply appreciate this sentiment. Picture this: you've just walked into a pitch meeting. Your idea is brilliant – it's innovative, it's fresh, and it's filling a gap that no one even knew existed. Yet, as you present, you can sense that the investors across the table are looking beyond your slides. Their probing questions, their discerning looks are aimed at understanding the people behind the idea. Because, in their seasoned minds, even a mediocre idea in the hands of a stellar team has the potential to turn to gold.

So, what makes a team stellar? It's not just about qualifications or impressive resumes. It's about a shared vision. When every member of your team wakes up with that burning desire to bring your collective dream to life, you're onto something special. It's this shared passion that turns challenges into stepping stones and setbacks into stories of perseverance.

But passion is just one piece of the puzzle. Diversity of thought and skill is another. In the world of startups, you need a blend of dreamers and doers. You need those who can paint the big picture and those who can dive deep into the minutiae. A strong team seamlessly marries these perspectives, ensuring that every decision is both visionary and grounded.

Adaptability, too, is crucial. The startup terrain is ever-shifting. Today's innovation can become obsolete tomorrow. It's the teams that not only anticipate these changes but also thrive in their midst, that truly stand out. This ability to pivot, to view change as an ally, is what separates fleeting successes from enduring legends.

Communication is the lifeblood of such teams. In my early days, I remember the transformative power of open dialogues. The brainstorming sessions that stretched into the wee hours, the candid feedback sessions, the moments of disagreement that led to breakthroughs – all these were possible because we fostered a culture where every voice mattered.

In your journey as a founder, you'll make countless decisions. But few will be as impactful as the people you choose to surround yourself with. As you set out to build your dream team, look beyond the obvious. Seek out passion, diversity, adaptability, and open-mindedness. Remember, the right team can elevate an average idea to greatness, but even the most groundbreaking idea might falter without the right hands steering its course.

To all the fellow founders out there: while your idea might light the way, it's the combined strength, tenacity, and brilliance of your team that will propel you to destinations unimagined. Cherish them, nurture them, and together, chart a course for the annals of startup success.

Crafting a Compelling Story

When I first embarked on my startup journey, armed with a product and a dream, I thought the hardest part would be the innovation itself. But as the days turned into months, I stumbled upon a realization that would redefine my entrepreneurial perspective: innovation alone doesn't guarantee success. Instead, it's the story behind that innovation, the narrative that wraps around your product and draws listeners into your world, that makes all the difference.

You see, fundraising isn't just about showcasing numbers or projections. At its core, it's a performance. Think about the last time you were utterly captivated by a movie or a novel. It wasn't just the plot that drew you in; it was the storytelling, the emotions it evoked, and the connection you felt with the characters. Similarly, when you stand before potential investors, you're not just pitching a business – you're unveiling a story. A story that needs to be so riveting, so compelling, that it convinces them to part with their hard-earned money and invest in your dream instead of letting it safely accrue interest in a bank.

But how does one craft such a tale? It starts with passion. You need to believe in your story deeply, for if you don't, how can you expect others to? Your narrative should echo your personal journey, the challenges faced, the breakthrough moments, and the vision that drives you. It's this raw, authentic emotion that forms the bedrock of a compelling narrative.

Next, weave in the problem you're solving. Every great story has conflict, and in the world of startups, this conflict is the market gap your product addresses. But don't just talk about the problem; paint a vivid picture of the world where this problem no longer exists because of your solution. This vision of a brighter future, one that's within reach because of your innovation, is what will ignite the spark in your audience.

Now, while passion and vision are critical, it's also essential to demonstrate the grit and resilience that have propelled your journey. Investors aren't just buying into a product; they're investing in the character and determination of the people behind it. Share anecdotes of setbacks turned into comebacks, of naysayers turned into advocates. Show them that you're not just a dreamer, but a relentless pursuer of that dream.

Lastly, always remember that every great story has a climax, a moment of revelation. For you, this is the transformative potential of your startup. It's the "mind-blowing" factor that sets you apart, that makes investors sit up and think, "I need to be a part of this."

My fellow founders, fundraising is more art than science. In this intricate dance of numbers and narratives, never underestimate the power of a captivating story. For it's not just capital you're after, but belief. And when you can make someone believe in your dream as fervently as you do, you're not just securing funds; you're gaining champions for your cause.

So, as you pen the next chapter of your startup journey, remember to craft it with care, passion, and authenticity. For in the world of business, where logic often reigns supreme, never forget the transformative magic of a well-told tale.

4. **The Different Stages of Fundraising**

Bootstrapping: Funding Yourself

There's a certain romance to the term "bootstrapping." It conjures images of rugged individualism, of pioneers forging paths through uncharted territories with nothing but their wits and willpower. And in the modern world of startups, this image isn't far from the truth.

I remember the early days of my venture, when the weight of every decision was solely on my shoulders. With limited funds and no external investors to answer to, I was truly the master of my ship. And let me tell you, there's an unparalleled freedom in that. The ability to chart your course, to pivot without seeking committee approvals, and to embrace your vision unapologetically.

However, as exhilarating as bootstrapping can be, it's also a journey marked by trials and tribulations. Without the safety net of external funding, every misstep feels amplified. Cash flow becomes a nightly concern, and resource allocation transforms into an art form. It's a balancing act of nurturing growth while ensuring the lights stay on.

But here's the beauty of bootstrapping: it teaches resilience like nothing else. Every dollar spent is a dollar earned, making you acutely aware of the value of hard work. It forces you to be scrappy, to think outside the box, to innovate not just in terms of your product but also in terms of your business model.

I've often been asked, "Why bootstrap when there's so much funding available out there?" And the answer, my fellow founders, lies in the essence of entrepreneurship itself. At the heart of every startup is a desire to solve a problem, to make a mark, to craft a legacy. And sometimes, the best way to stay true to this mission is to fund it yourself. It's about taking complete ownership, not just of the successes, but also of the failures and lessons they bring.

Bootstrapping also allows for an organic, customer-focused growth. Without the pressure of investor expectations, you can prioritize customer feedback, iterating and refining your product or service to perfection. It's a direct line to the market, unfiltered by external agendas.

Now, this isn't to say that bootstrapping is the only way, or even the best way, for every entrepreneur. But it is a path that offers invaluable lessons in self-reliance, adaptability, and perseverance.

To all the brave souls considering this journey, remember: bootstrapping might stretch you thin, but it also molds you into a robust and resourceful entrepreneur. The challenges are real, but so are the rewards. And when you look back, years down the line, at a successful empire built on sheer determination and grit, you'll cherish the memories of these early days, when every hurdle overcome was a personal triumph. In the vast landscape of startup stories, bootstrapping is your unique tale of tenacity, vision, and unwavering faith in yourself.

Friends and Family: Tapping Into Close Networks

Diving into the startup ecosystem feels a lot like stepping into the vastness of the open sea. The waters can be unpredictable, filled with both promising waves of opportunities and occasional storms of uncertainty. It's in these early, vulnerable stages that many of us consider seeking an anchor, something – or someone – familiar to offer support. For many entrepreneurs, that anchor is found among friends and family.

The choice to approach those closest to you for funding isn't merely a financial decision; it's deeply personal. I've walked that path, and let me share a little of what I've gleaned from my journey.

You see, when you turn to friends and family, you're not just presenting a business proposition. You're sharing a dream, a vision that you're deeply passionate about. These are the people who've been there through your ups and downs, who've seen you at your best and your worst, and who, more often than not, believe in you even when the world might be skeptical.

But this closeness, this inherent trust, is a double-edged sword. On one hand, these early believers invest not just in your idea, but in you. They've seen your dedication, your sleepless nights, and your relentless pursuit of your dream. Their faith often goes beyond market analyses or return on investments; it's rooted in a shared history and mutual respect.

However, with this faith comes a profound responsibility. The funds you acquire aren't faceless figures from distant investors; they come from your sister's savings, your best friend's paycheck, or your uncle's retirement fund. This intimate connection can amplify the pressure and make every business hiccup feel intensely personal.

But here's a perspective that I've grown to appreciate: this unique blend of professional and personal isn't a burden; it's a privilege. It's an opportunity to merge the worlds of business and relationships, to foster a community of supporters who are genuinely invested in your journey.

Still, a word of caution. When navigating these waters, transparency is paramount. Ensure that your loved ones understand the risks, and always, always prioritize open communication. Set clear boundaries, discuss expectations, and regularly update them on your progress. Remember, this isn't just about funding; it's about preserving relationships that are priceless.

The journey of incorporating friends and family into your startup narrative is nuanced, filled with moments of gratitude, bursts of inspiration, and bouts of anxiety. But when navigated with care, it can be one of the most rewarding experiences for an entrepreneur.

So, if you're contemplating this path, take a moment to appreciate the beauty of it all. In a world where business is often reduced to numbers and bottom lines, here's an avenue that celebrates human connection, trust, and shared dreams. It's a testament to the age-old adage: together, we go further.

Angel Investors: Early Believers in Your Vision

Ah, angel investors. The very term seems to conjure a sense of divine intervention, doesn't it? And for many of us on the startup journey, that's precisely how it feels. In the sprawling narrative of entrepreneurship, these individuals often step in at the most crucial chapters, offering not just capital but also faith in an idea that's still taking root.

I recall the first time I pitched to an angel investor. The anticipation, the nervous energy, the hope - it was a blend of emotions. These weren't faceless institutions or bureaucratic entities; they were real people who had been through the trenches themselves, understood the grind, and were now in a position to back the next wave of innovators.

Angel investors are unique creatures in the investment world. While they certainly aim for a return on their investment, their motivations often extend beyond the spreadsheet's cold calculations. Many have been founders themselves and know the mountains and valleys of building something from scratch. Their investment isn't just financial; it's emotional. They remember the taste of early setbacks and the thrill of initial traction. They've been in your shoes, and now, they're looking to give back, to play a part in the next big success story.

But as with any relationship, the bond between a founder and an angel investor is built on mutual trust and understanding. They're betting on you, yes, but it's more than that. They're entrusting you with their resources, their reputation, and a piece of their legacy. And in return, they offer not just capital but also mentorship, guidance, and a network that can open doors you didn't even know existed.

Now, while the allure of angel investment is undeniable, it's essential to remember that this is a partnership. Both sides come with expectations. As founders, we dream big, aiming for the stars. But it's equally vital to keep our feet on the ground, to understand our responsibilities, and to communicate openly. The best relationships with angel investors are built on transparency, mutual respect, and shared goals.

Looking back on my journey, some of the most pivotal moments came not from the funds that were infused into my venture but from the conversations, insights, and perspectives these early believers brought to the table. Their experiences, their triumphs, and even their mistakes became invaluable lessons for me.

To my fellow founders gearing up to engage with angel investors, remember this: Beyond the numbers, pitches, and negotiations lies an opportunity for a transformative partnership. It's a dance of dreams and pragmatism, passion and strategy. Embrace it, value it, and you'll find that these 'angels' offer a lot more than just wings for your venture. They offer heart, soul, and a shared journey towards the incredible.

Venture Capital: The Big Leagues

There comes a moment in the life of many startups when the horizon broadens. When the playgrounds of initial stages, filled with the familiarity of friends, family, and angel investors, start to seem a tad too small for the vast ambitions taking root. That's when many of us set our sights on venture capital, the big leagues of startup financing.

Venture capital (or VC, as it's colloquially known) isn't just another funding avenue; it's an ecosystem, a universe unto itself. I remember the first time I stepped into a VC firm's conference room. The aura was palpable. The walls seemed to resonate with stories of startups that had become industry behemoths, ideas that had transformed markets, and founders who had rewritten the rules of the game.

Venture capitalists operate on a scale that's often transformative. They aren't just looking for solid businesses; they're scouting for potential unicorns, companies that could redefine industries and offer exponential returns. This level of investment can propel startups to heights they hadn't dared to dream of. But, and it's a significant but, it comes with its unique set of challenges and expectations.

When VCs invest, they're not just putting money on the line; they're investing their firm's reputation, their expertise, and their expansive network. Their stakes are high, and naturally, their expectations match that intensity. They're looking for founders who exhibit a rare blend of vision, adaptability, and tenacity. Founders who not only dream but have the grit to make those dreams a reality.

It's easy to be swayed by the allure of venture capital – the large fundings, the flashy headlines, and the success stories. But, dear founders, venture capital is not just about the money. It's a partnership, a commitment to scale and evolve, and sometimes, a pledge to pivot when required. It's about aligning visions and combining forces to chase shared goals. It's about rigorous board meetings, challenging questions, and late-night strategy sessions.

Navigating the world of VCs requires a balance. On one side, there's the undeniable thrill of scaling, of taking your startup to the global stage. On the other, there's the weight of responsibility, the understanding that the stakes have multiplied. Every decision, every move now impacts a broader set of stakeholders.

Yet, in this intricate dance of ambition and accountability, there's an underlying beauty. VCs, with their vast experience and industry insights, can be invaluable mentors. Their networks can open doors you didn't even know were there. Their expertise can guide you through market intricacies and operational challenges. They don't just fund your journey; in many ways, they become co-travelers, invested as deeply in your dream as you are.

In my tryst with venture capital, I've learned, grown, faltered, and soared. It's been a roller coaster, no doubt, but also an adventure of a lifetime. So, to those of you on the cusp of this journey, I offer this – venture capital is as much about the venture as it is about the capital. Embrace the ride, learn from every twist and turn, and remember, in the big leagues, it's not just about playing the game, but elevating it.

Corporate Investment and Strategic Partnerships

Entering the realm of corporate investment and strategic partnerships feels akin to being a promising young athlete and suddenly getting drafted into the major leagues. The stage is grander, the audience more vast, and the players—well, they're some of the biggest names in the industry. It's a thrilling, heady feeling, but it also requires a new game plan.

I recall the first time my startup engaged with a corporate investor. We were no longer in the world of pitch decks and accelerators. Instead, we found ourselves navigating boardrooms filled with executives who had been steering industry giants for years. Their language was different—terms like "synergy," "strategic alignment," and "long-term value creation" took center stage.

Corporate investment is not just about injecting funds into your startup; it's a statement. It says that an established entity sees potential in what you've built and believes in its place within the broader industry landscape. This validation is invigorating. But with it comes the realization that you're no longer just responsible for your vision, but also for how it aligns with and adds value to this corporate entity's vast operations.

Then there's the magic of strategic partnerships. These alliances are about more than money; they're about leveraging combined strengths. A well-orchestrated partnership can open doors to new markets, provide access to critical resources, or even streamline operational bottlenecks. In essence, it's two entities coming together, saying, "Together, we can achieve more."

However, while the allure of corporate investment and strategic partnerships is undeniable, it's essential to approach them with clarity and caution. These are not just financial transactions; they're relationships, often long-term ones. The key lies in ensuring alignment—not just in terms of business objectives but also in culture, vision, and growth trajectories.

It's tempting to view corporate entities as monolithic giants, but remember, they're made up of people. Just like us. People who are passionate, driven, and invested in crafting success stories. During my first significant partnership negotiation, I was struck by how similar our aspirations were, despite the difference in scale. They wanted innovation, growth, and success—just like we did.

Corporate partnerships have enriched my entrepreneurial journey in ways I hadn't imagined. They've offered insights into industry dynamics, provided a macro perspective, and often, taught me the value of patience in business. But, most importantly, they've reinforced the idea that entrepreneurship is not a solitary journey. It's a collective endeavor, made richer through collaboration, shared dreams, and mutual growth.

So, to my fellow founders on the brink of exploring corporate investment and partnerships, here's my two cents: Embrace the scale, but cherish the relationship. Understand the terms, but value the human connection. Dive into the vastness of the corporate world, but never lose sight of your core values. In this dance of startups and giants, when done right, both can lead and follow, creating a harmony that's truly exhilarating.

5. **Pitching to Investors**

Crafting the Perfect Pitch Deck

I still remember the first time I sat down to create a pitch deck for my startup. With a blank PowerPoint slide staring back at me, it felt like standing at the base of Everest, pondering the arduous climb ahead. The questions swirling in my mind were many: How do I condense my vision, passion, and months (or even years) of hard work into a few slides? How do I make it compelling, concise, yet comprehensive?

As I grappled with these questions, a piece of advice from a seasoned entrepreneur friend came to mind: "Don't reinvent the wheel." The startup ecosystem is one of shared journeys. Countless founders have walked this path, faced similar challenges, and found unique solutions. And many, in a gesture of camaraderie, have made their pitch decks public, offering a glimpse into their strategic thinking and storytelling prowess.

There's a certain humility in understanding that you don't always have to start from scratch. Especially when crafting something as pivotal as a pitch deck. It's perfectly alright to draw inspiration from those who've come before you. In fact, I'd argue it's smart. While every startup's story is unique, the core elements that investors look for often remain consistent. By studying successful pitch decks, you not only understand these elements but also how best to present them.

Now, I'm not saying you should just replicate another company's deck slide by slide. That would do a disservice to your unique journey and vision. But borrowing structural cues, design elements, or even the flow of storytelling can give you a solid foundation to build upon.

There's an art and science to crafting a compelling pitch deck. The art lies in telling your story in a way that resonates, that pulls at heartstrings while also making logical sense. The science, on the other hand, is about understanding the nuances of what makes a pitch deck effective: the right data points, the balance between vision and traction, and the subtle interplay between confidence and humility.

But here's a little secret, dear founders: Your pitch deck is not just for investors. It's for you. It's a mirror that reflects your clarity of thought, your understanding of the market, and your roadmap ahead. It's a tool that helps distill your expansive vision into actionable steps. And every time you present it, it becomes a reaffirmation of your commitment to this journey.

So, while it's okay (and often wise) to borrow from the successes of others, always infuse your deck with your essence. Let it be a testament to your passion, your grit, and your unique perspective. Because, in the end, while a pitch deck might be a tool for fundraising, it's the authenticity behind it that truly makes investors believe.

In this journey of entrepreneurship, we stand on the shoulders of giants. Let's learn from them, draw from their wisdom, but always, always remember to add our chapter to the story.

The Elevator Pitch: Making an Impression in Minutes

The elevator pitch. It's a term you've undoubtedly heard, tossed around in entrepreneurial circles and startup workshops. But until you've actually found yourself in that confined space, with just a few floors to sell your life's passion, you might not truly grasp its weight.

I remember my first unscheduled elevator pitch vividly. The doors slid shut, and there I was, side by side with a potential investor I'd been trying to get a meeting with for months. My heart raced. I had, what, 30 seconds? A minute at most? It was showtime.

Now, let me share something. In that brief encounter, I learned that the elevator pitch isn't just about selling a business idea; it's about presenting a vision, a passion, and a mission succinctly and compellingly. It's about capturing the essence of countless sleepless nights, strategic pivots, and lessons learned, all within the span of a few breaths.

Some might argue that boiling down the intricacies of your startup into such a condensed format is an oversimplification. But I've come to see it as an art form. It's about discernment — knowing what truly matters and being able to communicate that with conviction and clarity.

What's fascinating about the elevator pitch is that it's not just about those unexpected moments in elevators. It's about cocktail parties, brief encounters at networking events, or even bumping into an old friend at a cafe who might just know someone interested in what you're doing. The world is teeming with opportunities, and having a crisp, engaging elevator pitch ensures you're always ready to seize them.

Crafting this pitch requires introspection. It forces you to cut through the noise and ask, "What is the core of what I'm doing? Why should anyone care? And why now?" It's about distilling your startup's essence into its purest form and then sharing it with infectious enthusiasm.

To my fellow founders, I'd say this: Don't be daunted by the elevator pitch. Embrace it as a challenge, as a tool that hones your vision and sharpens your focus. Rehearse it, refine it, but also let it evolve as your startup does.

And when that moment comes, when the universe conspires to put you in the same confined space with someone who could change your startup's trajectory, breathe deep, smile, and speak your truth. Because you never know — that brief elevator ride might just be the ascent your startup has been waiting for.

Navigating Q&A Sessions

One might think that after wrapping up a meticulously crafted presentation, the hard part is over. I used to believe that too, until I stood before a room full of potential investors during my first Q&A session. Suddenly, the spotlight wasn't just on my slides or the numbers; it was on me, my knowledge, my adaptability, and my passion.

Q&A sessions are a different beast altogether. It's where the facade fades, and raw, unscripted moments take the stage. It's also where some of the most profound connections with investors are forged. They're not just asking questions about your startup; they're probing your depth as a founder, your understanding of the landscape, and your vision's resilience.

The first time I was peppered with questions ranging from the intricacies of our business model to our five-year plan, I felt like I was navigating a minefield. But with each answer, with each moment of vulnerability or affirmation, I realized I was painting a more holistic and authentic picture of our journey.

Here's what I've gleaned from numerous Q&A sessions over the years: It's not about having all the answers; it's about how you handle the questions. There will be times when you might not know the answer, and that's okay. What matters is your willingness to acknowledge it, your commitment to finding out, and your ability to pivot the conversation back to your vision.

But it's also an opportunity, a golden one at that. Through these questions, investors are inadvertently showing you areas of potential concern or facets of your business you might not have delved deeply into. It's feedback, raw and immediate. Embrace it.

To my fellow founders, navigating a Q&A session is as much about listening as it is about speaking. Hear the unsaid in their questions. Is there an underlying concern about scalability? Do they need more clarity on your market positioning? Listen, adapt, and respond.

And remember, each question is an open door, an invitation to reinforce your narrative, to address doubts, and to showcase the depth of your commitment and understanding.

In the end, Q&A sessions are less about the barrage of questions and more about the bridges you build with your responses. They're opportunities in disguise, moments where the unscripted, authentic you can shine the brightest. Embrace them, learn from them, and let them refine not just your pitch but your journey as a founder.

Common Pitch Mistakes and How to Avoid Them

The journey of pitching is fraught with bumps and turns. Even the most seasoned founders can tell you about a pitch that went sideways. And I'm no exception. Reflecting on my experiences and the countless pitches I've given, witnessed, and received feedback on, it's evident that certain missteps are more common than others. Today, I want to shine a light on these pitfalls not as a cautionary tale, but as a roadmap to guide you towards a successful pitch.

1. Overselling and Underselling. It's a delicate balance. In my early days, filled with unbridled enthusiasm, I'd find myself overselling, making grand promises and using superlatives at every turn. But soon I realized that while passion is essential, credibility is paramount. On the flip side, underselling your vision because of humility or fear of coming on too strong can be equally detrimental. The key is to find that sweet spot, where confidence meets authenticity.

2. Ignoring the Audience. I remember one particular pitch where I was so engrossed in my slides that I failed to notice the investor's eyes glazing over. I was talking *at* them, not *to* them. It's crucial to read the room, adjust your tone, and perhaps even pivot your presentation based on their reactions. Remember, it's a dialogue, not a monologue.

3. Getting Lost in the Weeds. In an attempt to showcase our expertise, we sometimes delve deep into the technicalities. While it's important to show you know your stuff, overwhelming your audience with jargon or intricacies can make them lose sight of your vision. Keep it high-level, with the option to dive deeper if prompted.

4. Not Addressing the Elephant in the Room. Let's face it; every startup has challenges, and investors know this. They're not just looking for opportunities; they're scouting for potential risks. Instead of shying away from these, address them head-on. By highlighting challenges and your strategies to overcome them, you not only display transparency but also foresight.

5. Neglecting the 'Why Now'. Why is this the moment for your startup to shine? In my pitches, I've learned that painting the bigger picture, setting the stage with current market dynamics, trends, and shifts can create a compelling argument for the timeliness and relevance of your solution.

Pitching is an art. But like all art forms, it's constantly evolving. What remains consistent, however, is the need for clarity, connection, and conviction. For every mistake I've shared, there are countless success stories, tales of founders who've learned, adapted, and emerged stronger.

To all the founders out there, I want to leave you with this: Every pitch, every interaction, is a learning experience. Take the feedback, reflect on it, and use it as fuel to refine your narrative. In the world of startups, resilience isn't just a virtue; it's a necessity. And remember, every 'no' is one step closer to that exhilarating 'yes'. Embrace the journey.

6. **The Mistakes Not to Make When Talking to an Investor**

First Impressions and Their Lasting Impact

There's an age-old adage, "You never get a second chance to make a first impression." Having walked the tightrope of startup life and stood in countless rooms with potential partners, clients, and investors, I can affirm the profound truth behind this saying. The initial moments, the first exchanges, they set the stage. And in the world of startups, where the landscape shifts rapidly and opportunities are fleeting, those early impressions can be monumental.

I recall an early meeting with a potential investor. It was one of those big ones, the kind where the stakes are high, and the room's energy is palpable. I'd prepared extensively, rehearsed my lines, and felt confident in our proposal. Yet, as the discussion kicked off, I noticed a subtle shift. It wasn't in the content of my presentation or the numbers. It was in the nuances — the firmness of a handshake, the attentiveness during introductions, the readiness to engage in a spontaneous conversation before diving into the pitch.

That day, I learned that first impressions go beyond just what you're presenting. They encompass the entire aura you bring into a space: your demeanor, your attentiveness, and, most importantly, your authenticity.

But why are these first impressions so incredibly crucial, especially in the startup world?

For one, in a landscape saturated with innovation and a plethora of brilliant ideas, it's the people behind these ideas that often become the differentiators. Investors, clients, and partners are not just investing in a product or service; they're investing in you, the founder, and your team. That initial impression becomes a reflection of your brand, your ethos, and your commitment.

Moreover, the startup journey is rife with challenges. When potential stakeholders meet you, they're assessing whether you're someone they can weather storms with. Can they trust you during turbulent times? Your demeanor, your confidence, and the respect with which you engage become indicators of the partnership's potential longevity.

I've often been asked, "How do you craft a lasting first impression?" While there's no one-size-fits-all answer, the foundation lies in authenticity. Be genuine in your interactions, be present in the moment, and listen actively. Every interaction is a two-way street. While you aim to leave an imprint, be receptive to the impressions others leave on you.

To my fellow founders: As you navigate this exhilarating, challenging, and rewarding world of startups, remember that while your product, service, or solution will evolve, the impressions you leave in these initial moments become a part of your story's fabric. They have the power to open doors or close them. So, walk into each room with purpose, authenticity, and the knowledge that every handshake, every exchange, is an opportunity to leave a legacy.

Reading the Room: Gauging Investor Interest

There's a certain electricity in the air when you're about to present your startup vision to a room full of potential investors. It's a mix of excitement, anticipation, and, of course, those jitters that remind you of just how much is at stake. But one of the skills I've found most invaluable during these high-pressure moments isn't just delivering a pitch — it's the ability to 'read the room.'

Now, let me share a little story from my early days. I was in a sleek, high-rise building downtown, about to present to a group of investors who, frankly, could make or break our next phase. As I dove into the presentation, I noticed one investor continuously checking his watch, another seemingly lost in thought, staring out of the window. It wasn't hard to feel a tinge of discouragement. But then, I took a moment, took a deep breath, and shifted my approach. Instead of barreling through the slides, I paused and threw out an unexpected question to the group, bringing the wandering minds back to the present. And that made all the difference.

Being attuned to your audience's reactions, their body language, and even the subtle shifts in energy can give you insights that no amount of preparation can. It tells you when to dive deeper into a point, when to pull back, and when to engage directly to recapture interest.

But how do you develop this skill of reading the room?

Start by being hyper-aware. Take note of who leans in when you're discussing specific aspects of your business and who takes notes. These are often positive signs of interest. Conversely, frequent distractions, like checking phones or whispered side conversations, can indicate waning engagement or even skepticism.

Remember, every investor is unique. While one might be searching for market-size numbers that make their eyes light up, another might be more interested in your go-to-market strategy or the technical prowess of your solution. By being attuned to these nuances, you can tailor your conversation on the fly, addressing the unique interests and concerns of those in the room.

And, sometimes, gauging interest isn't just about what happens during the presentation. The questions posed afterward, the nature of the follow-up, and the eagerness (or lack thereof) in their voices can also be indicative of their interest levels.

To my fellow founders, as you venture into these critical meetings, remember that your ability to connect, to engage, and to read the room can be just as influential as the business model or the innovation you're presenting. Because, in the end, investments aren't just about numbers or projections; they're about relationships, trust, and shared visions. So, as you stand in that room, be present, be attuned, and most importantly, be ready to pivot, engage, and connect in ways that resonate with those who hold the keys to your startup's next chapter.

Y Combinator's Advice

In the dynamic world of startups, Y Combinator stands as a beacon of wisdom, inspiration, and mentorship. For those unfamiliar, Y Combinator is one of the premier startup accelerators globally, having guided many fledgling companies into industry giants. Having had the privilege to glean insights from their trove of expertise, I felt compelled to share some of their invaluable advice that's resonated deeply with me and many other founders.

You know, when you first dip your toes into the chaotic waters of entrepreneurship, you're often bombarded with advice from every direction. Some good, some not so much. But when Y Combinator speaks, you listen. Why? Because they've been through the trenches, seen the patterns, and possess a keen understanding of what truly matters in the startup world.

One of the first gems I picked up from them was the principle of "Make Something People Want." It sounds simple enough, right? Yet, so many startups get wrapped up in their innovative solutions and intricate technologies that they lose sight of the most critical stakeholder: the user. If there's no genuine need or want for what you're offering, no amount of marketing magic can save you. Being obsessed with user needs, continuously iterating based on feedback, and prioritizing user experience above all else is crucial.

Another pivotal insight revolves around focus. In the initial stages, it's easy to be pulled in a million directions. Y Combinator emphasizes the importance of zeroing in on what truly matters and relentlessly pursuing that. Especially in the early days, when resources are limited, spreading yourself too thin can be the death knell for your venture.

Then there's the ethos of resilience. The startup journey is rife with challenges, setbacks, and failures. It's par for the course. Y Combinator stresses the need for grit, for pushing through when things seem bleak, and for viewing failures as learning opportunities rather than roadblocks.

Lastly, and perhaps most profoundly, they often highlight the value of community. Surrounding yourself with other like-minded founders, sharing struggles, triumphs, and insights can be transformative. It's not just about networking; it's about mutual support, understanding, and camaraderie.

To all my fellow founders, as we navigate our unique paths, it's insights like these from Y Combinator that can serve as our North Star. While every journey is unique, and while not every piece of advice will apply universally, the wisdom of those who've been there and done that can be an invaluable compass. So, as we push forward, let's remember to stay user-focused, remain resilient, prioritize our efforts, and cherish the community we're a part of. Because together, we can turn visions into realities.

Balancing Honesty and Optimism

Ah, the delicate dance between honesty and optimism. It's something every founder grapples with, especially when facing potential investors. On one hand, we're told to "sell the dream," to paint a rosy picture of the future that gets people excited to be a part of the journey. On the other hand, we understand the inherent value of honesty, of laying out the challenges and uncertainties that lie ahead.

From my own journey, and after countless pitches and meetings, I've come to realize that this balance isn't just about making a sale; it's about building trust, forming genuine partnerships, and setting the stage for long-term success.

Let's be real for a moment: startups are inherently risky. The statistics on startup failures are commonly cited, often casting a shadow over even the most upbeat pitch presentations. Yet, if all we did was focus on the pitfalls, we'd never inspire confidence or attract the partnerships needed to grow and thrive. This is where optimism comes into play.

But optimism isn't about ignoring the challenges or sugar-coating the truth. It's about framing those challenges as opportunities. It's about showcasing the team's capability to navigate the treacherous waters of entrepreneurship. It's about believing in the mission and vision, even in the face of adversity.

On the flip side, blatant over-promising or brushing over significant obstacles can erode investor trust. I've sat across from investors whose piercing questions revealed a depth of experience and insight that you just can't fool. And honestly, you wouldn't want to. These are the partners who, when they commit, will be with you through thick and thin. They don't just buy into a product or service; they buy into you, the founder. Your integrity, your vision, and your ability to lead.

So, how does one strike the balance?

Start by being upfront about the challenges. Show that you've thought deeply about potential obstacles, from market fluctuations to competitive pressures. But, just as quickly as you lay out these challenges, pivot to the strategies and approaches you're employing to tackle them. This showcases both awareness and proactive thinking.

And, perhaps most importantly, weave a narrative of resilience. Share stories from your own entrepreneurial journey or those of your team, highlighting moments of overcoming odds or turning challenges into advantages. Investors love a good comeback story – not because it's dramatic, but because it speaks to tenacity, adaptability, and drive.

In the end, remember that both honesty and optimism are crucial. They're two sides of the same coin, working in tandem to build trust, inspire confidence, and pave the way for fruitful partnerships. As founders, our task is to master the art of weaving them together into a compelling, authentic narrative.

7. **Navigating Global Investment Landscapes: Unraveling the Distinctiveness of US, European, MENA, and Asian Investors**

US Investors: The Hub of Innovation

The United States has often been hailed as a beacon for startups and innovation. From the bustling streets of New York to the tech-driven atmosphere of Silicon Valley, it seems there's an entrepreneurial spirit in the very air we breathe here. But what makes US investors unique, and what should you, as a founder, understand about navigating the landscape of American venture capital?

When I first started my journey as an entrepreneur, I was astounded by the scale and breadth of opportunities in the US. The sheer volume of capital available and the established ecosystem for startups is unlike anywhere else. Many of the world's most renowned venture capital firms call the US home, and there's a reason for that.

Economically, the US has a robust framework for startups. The country's capital markets are vast, offering varied funding stages, from seed to IPO. This has been cultivated over decades, with both public and private sectors playing vital roles in fostering a conducive environment for business growth. In fact, the SEC's approach to regulation, while ensuring investor protection, also facilitates fundraising, especially with mechanisms like the JOBS Act that opened doors for crowdfunding.

Yet, it's not just about the money. US investors tend to prioritize innovation and scalability. They're on the lookout for startups that don't just solve a problem but have the potential to redefine industries. This mindset is rooted in a history of American enterprises, from Ford to Apple, which didn't just succeed in business — they revolutionized their fields.

However, there's also a cultural layer to understand. American business culture is direct, and while it values vision, there's a strong emphasis on metrics, milestones, and execution. Investors here appreciate clarity and brevity, so when you're pitching, be ready to get straight to the point.

But let's touch upon the element of inclusiveness. The US, often termed a melting pot, houses diverse cultures, backgrounds, and experiences. While this is one of its greatest strengths, it's essential to approach it with sensitivity. Recognize the vast diversity within the nation, and ensure that you are not making assumptions about a homogenized "American" culture. Each region, from the East Coast to the West, the Midwest to the South, brings its own nuances and values.

In recent years, there's been a commendable push towards more inclusive investing, with a rise in funds dedicated to supporting underrepresented founders. This is a testament to the ever-evolving landscape of US investing, one that acknowledges its shortcomings and is actively working towards a more equitable future.

In conclusion, the US offers a rich tapestry of opportunities for startups. Yet, like any landscape, it has its intricacies. By understanding both the economic mechanisms and the cultural nuances, you can position yourself for a successful fundraising journey in the hub of innovation.

European Investors: A Diverse Investment Climate

Europe is buzzing. For years, the startup spotlight predominantly focused on tech titans from the US. But recently, there's been a marked shift. Europe, with its rich tapestry of cultures and histories, is not only emerging from the shadows but is increasingly claiming center stage in the global startup arena.

When we think about the European startup ecosystem, traditionally, the UK and Germany might come to mind. These nations have undoubtedly been powerhouses in cultivating tech talent and fostering innovation. Yet, the winds of change are blowing, bringing with them an exciting era of diversification within the European investment landscape.

Of particular note is the rise of countries that were previously less recognized on the global startup scene. France, for instance, has been making waves with remarkable ventures like BlaBlaCar, showcasing its potential as a hub for entrepreneurial success. Similarly, Italy, often celebrated for its rich art and history, has taken the tech world by surprise, particularly with the outstanding success of Contents.com.

So, what's behind this dynamic shift? A myriad of factors. One of the most palpable is a renewed entrepreneurial spirit and ambition. Gone are the days when European startups solely aimed to conquer their domestic market. Today's visionaries from Paris to Rome are dreaming big, aiming to make a global impact.

European governments have caught onto this momentum, rolling out the red carpet for startups with pro-business policies, significant tax breaks, and innovation-friendly regulations. This kind of governmental support is helping cities like Milan or Marseille stand toe-to-toe with established hubs like Berlin.

Yet, while the financial and policy frameworks are essential, it's the unique European cultural fabric that provides an added edge. There's an emphasis on building genuine relationships, a celebration of diverse perspectives, and a deep-rooted appreciation for work-life balance. These cultural nuances, when combined with sheer ambition, are creating a potent mix that investors find hard to resist.

However, it's paramount to approach this vast landscape with an open mind. Europe's strength lies in its diversity. Each nation, be it Spain with its fiery entrepreneurial spirit or Finland with its focus on sustainable tech, offers something unique.

In conclusion, Europe's startup ecosystem is evolving rapidly. With nations like Italy and France rising to prominence alongside traditional heavyweights, the continent offers a world of opportunities for founders. As this narrative unfolds, it's becoming increasingly clear that Europe's startup story, rich in tradition and brimming with potential, has many more chapters left to write.

MENA Investors: Emerging Markets and Growth Opportunities

The Middle East and North Africa, or MENA as it's frequently referred to, offers a rich mosaic of economic landscapes. While this region might be historically known for its opulence derived from oil, it's now making waves for a different reason: a burgeoning startup ecosystem that's catching the attention of global investors.

It's an exciting time to witness the transformation of this region. Places like Dubai, often synonymous with luxury and oil wealth, are now becoming epicenters for innovation. It's not just the gleaming skyscrapers that stand tall; now, young companies, driven by passionate founders and fueled by unique ideas, are making their mark. The shift is palpable, and as someone who's been through the startup grind, I can attest to the energy that's currently coursing through MENA's business veins.

But what's really intriguing is the source of this change. The immense oil reserves, which once kept these economies buoyant, are now serving a new purpose. Saudi Arabia, for instance, through its Vision 2030, is channeling a significant portion of its oil revenue towards technology and innovation. It's not just about diversifying their economy but also about acknowledging that the future lies beyond oil. For startups, this means a vast sea of funds waiting to be tapped into, with investors keenly looking for the next big idea.

However, while the opportunity is vast, it's essential to approach it with cultural sensitivity. Each country in the MENA region has its own intricacies, traditions, and business etiquettes. As founders, while we might be bursting with excitement about our product or solution, it's equally crucial to understand and respect the local norms.

And yet, the common thread that binds these nations is a shared enthusiasm for growth and innovation. The young population, increased internet penetration, and a government keen on nurturing startups are creating the perfect storm for unprecedented growth. For founders looking to make an impact, MENA isn't just an emerging market; it's the future.

Remember, the MENA region offers more than just funding. It presents a chance to collaborate, understand different perspectives, and truly go global. The key is to balance ambition with empathy, innovation with respect.
Asian Investors: The Powerhouses of the East

Asia, with its vast expanse and diverse cultures, has always been an enchanting mystery to the West. But in the business world, especially in the startup ecosystem, Asia is no longer just a land of age-old traditions and mesmerizing landscapes. It's become a powerhouse, a nerve center of innovation and investment that's reshaping the global economic landscape.

Let's take a moment to understand the scale of what we're talking about. From the bustling streets of Bangalore to the sophisticated boardrooms of Tokyo, from the innovative hubs of Shenzhen to the dynamic marketplaces of Singapore, Asia is pulsating with entrepreneurial energy. This region is home to some of the world's most prominent tech giants and unicorns, and they're not just competing on a local scale but are setting global standards.

But what makes Asia such an attractive proposition for startup founders like us? For one, the region boasts a blend of mature markets like Japan and South Korea, along with rapidly growing economies such as India and Vietnam. This presents a spectrum of opportunities, from tapping into established consumer bases to introducing innovations in markets eager for disruption.

However, what genuinely stands out is the mindset of Asian investors. They're not just looking for the next big tech breakthrough. They appreciate the intricate balance of innovation, scalability, and sustainability. They understand the nuances of local markets and yet have a vision that transcends borders. For founders, this means access to capital that's backed by a deep understanding of regional dynamics.

Still, just as with any venture, it's crucial to approach the Asian investment scene with a keen awareness of its diversity. While the potential is immense, so are the cultural, economic, and regulatory differences between countries. Each nation has its own unique business etiquette, consumer behavior, and market challenges. And while the language of innovation is universal, the key to success in Asia lies in understanding and embracing these nuances.

In closing, if there's one thing I'd want fellow founders to take away from this, it's that Asia is more than just an investment destination. It's a mosaic of opportunities, insights, and collaborations. In this ever-shrinking world, looking Eastward might just be the move that propels your startup into the global limelight. So, gear up, do your homework, and dive into the vibrant tapestry that is Asia. Your next big breakthrough might just be waiting around the corner.

8. **Valuation and Term Sheets**

Determining Your Startup's Worth

Ah, the age-old conundrum of valuing a startup. Every founder, at some point, wrestles with that burning question: What's my company truly worth? You see, placing a value on a startup is as much art as it is science, a blend of number-crunching and gut instinct. But let me let you in on a little secret: sometimes, smaller is better. Shocked? Let me explain.

In the throes of the excitement that comes with seeing your brainchild grow, there's an almost irresistible temptation to aim for the stars with your valuations. We live in an age where billion-dollar valuations make headlines, but they also carry a weight that not every founder understands.

Imagine for a moment that you've just secured a funding round at a whopping billion-dollar valuation. It's exhilarating. The world seems to be at your feet. But with that valuation comes a set of expectations, a pressure-cooker environment where anything less than astronomical growth might be seen as a failure. If you've been valued at a billion, selling for anything less seems, in many ways, like falling short. And believe me, that's a pressure you might not want.

On the other hand, let's consider a more modest valuation, say $10 million. This doesn't have the same flashiness as a unicorn status, but here's the magic: it's sustainable. It allows for organic growth, for setting achievable milestones without the looming cloud of unrealistic expectations. If you've been valued at $10 million, and then you get an offer to sell at $20 million? That's a resounding success story.

But more than just the numbers, it's about the narrative you're creating. A grounded valuation tells investors that you're pragmatic, that you understand the market, and that you're building for the long run, not just the headlines. It signals sustainability, maturity, and a keen understanding of the intricate dance of startup growth.

So, my fellow founders, as you stand on the precipice of that all-important valuation decision, I urge you to take a step back. Look beyond the glitz and glamour of sky-high numbers. Think sustainability, think growth, but most importantly, think about the legacy you want to leave behind. Because, at the end of the day, it's not about how high you valued today, but how you grow, thrive, and make a difference tomorrow.

Understanding and Negotiating Term Sheets

If there's one phase in the startup journey that's akin to playing chess, it's the dance of negotiation, especially when term sheets come into play. And let me tell you, my fellow founders, this is not the time to cut corners. This is the arena where experience, foresight, and strategic acumen make all the difference. Your move here determines your startup's future, your stake in the game, and in many ways, the trajectory of your dream. And to make the right move, sometimes, you've got to bring in the grandmasters: top-tier lawyers.

I get it, starting up is all about cost-cutting, making do with what you have, and often being frugal to stretch every dollar. But when it comes to term sheets, frugality can cost you much more than you'd ever save. Why? Because investors, especially seasoned ones, have sat across the table many times, armed with legal teams whose sole job is to ensure the best deal for them. And unless you have someone equally adept on your side, you're entering a gunfight armed with a spoon.

You see, a term sheet, though non-binding, is the foundation upon which your entire investment deal is built. It defines everything: how much control you'll retain, how profits and losses will be divided, what happens if things go south, and what's expected of both parties. These are not simple agreements; they are intricate contracts filled with legal jargon and clauses that can have long-lasting implications.

I've witnessed too many passionate founders, brimming with ideas and enthusiasm, get sidelined because they didn't fully grasp the nuances of their term sheets. They thought they were getting a good deal, only to realize much later that they'd signed away more than they'd intended. And by then? It's often too late.

So, here's my sincere advice to you: invest in the best legal counsel you can afford when diving into term sheets. View it not as an expense, but as an investment in your startup's future. Because, at the end of the day, you want a fair deal, one that respects both your vision and the investor's stake. And that, dear founders, is achieved not by hoping for the best, but by preparing for it.

Key Clauses to Watch Out For

In the high-stakes world of startup fundraising, one can't stress enough the importance of details. It's those small print clauses, those seemingly innocuous terms that can make or break a deal—and potentially your startup's future. In your journey as a founder, the term sheet can be both your shield and sword, but only if you understand it in-depth. So, while I'd always advocate for hiring top-notch legal counsel to guide you (trust me on this, it pays off), it's equally crucial for you as a founder to be well-versed with some key clauses. Here's a primer to get you started:

- **Liquidation Preference:** This specifies the order in which shareholders get paid if the company is sold or liquidated. Sounds simple, right? But the specifics matter. A 1x liquidation preference means investors get their money back before others. Anything more than that, and they're taking a bigger piece of the pie.

- **Anti-dilution Provisions:** If you issue shares at a lower price in the future, this clause protects investors by adjusting their share price. But be wary — there are variations, and not understanding them can erode your ownership faster than you'd think.

- **Vesting:** It's about how your shares as a founder 'mature' over time. Standard vesting is usually over four years, but investors might push for different timelines. This is your sweat and blood we're talking about, so ensure you're comfortable with the timelines.

- **Board Composition:** Who gets to sit at the decision-making table? While it's typical for investors to seek board seats, be cautious about giving away too much control.

- **Drag-Along Rights:** This clause can compel minority shareholders to sell their shares in certain circumstances. While it ensures unity in a sale, ensure it's fair and not overly restrictive.

- **Right of First Refusal (ROFR):** If you, as a founder, decide to sell your shares, this gives investors the first dibs to buy them. Not necessarily bad, but be clear on the terms.

- **No-Shop Clause:** It restricts you from shopping your startup to other investors for a specified period. It's like dating exclusively, so ensure the duration is something you're comfortable with.

In the labyrinth of legalese, it's easy to get lost. That's why, as I always say, hire the best lawyers. Their experience will illuminate the path, ensuring you don't trip over hidden pitfalls. But beyond that, equip yourself with knowledge. Remember, in the game of startups, the more you know, the less likely you are to be taken by surprise. And that, my fellow founders, can make all the difference.

9. **The Due Diligence Process**

What Investors Are Looking For: The Due Diligence Dance

So, you've caught an investor's eye. Congratulations! But before they write that check, there's a critical phase you'll need to navigate: due diligence. It's a term that might sound formal and a tad intimidating, but at its core, it's the investor doing their homework to ensure they're making a sound decision.

Now, I'll be candid with you, my fellow founders. Due diligence isn't a mere formality. It's the investor's deep dive into every facet of your business. It's their opportunity to probe, question, and dissect, to get to the very heart of what makes your startup tick. They'll explore everything: from your financials, market positioning, to your team's background and capabilities.

Your financial health will be scrutinized. They'll look for red flags in your balance sheets, assess the sustainability of your revenue streams, and evaluate your burn rate. Investors want to ensure their investment won't evaporate in a business model with no clear path to profitability.

But here's a perspective shift: this isn't just about them. Due diligence is a two-way street. It's a chance for you to understand your potential investors better. How do they work with their portfolio companies? Are they hands-on or hands-off? What's their track record in helping startups scale?

However, there's a caveat. This process, thorough as it is, can sometimes feel invasive. And here's where my piece of advice comes in, one that I've learned from hard-won experience: always have the best legal team by your side. Believe me, it's worth every penny. With seasoned lawyers on your team, you're not only safeguarding your interests but also ensuring you understand every clause, every implication.

In essence, due diligence is the rigorous process where both parties assess fit. Investors are ensuring your startup is a worthy vessel for their capital, and you're ensuring that this investor aligns with your vision and can truly add value beyond just dollars. So, while it may feel intense, it's the foundation of a successful, symbiotic relationship. And remember, with the right legal counsel, you're not just navigating this phase – you're mastering it.

Preparing Your Business for Scrutiny

There's an old saying: "Sunlight is the best disinfectant." Now, while that usually refers to the importance of transparency in public affairs, it's surprisingly apt for startups, too. As founders, we often liken our ventures to our 'babies' – and who would ever want to admit that their baby might have blemishes? But here's the deal: when you're seeking investments, that sunlight is going to shine on your business. It's going to reveal everything - the good, the bad, and the in-between.

I know the journey. There you are, hustling, grinding, and wearing a dozen hats every day. Your company is moving so fast, and amidst that chaos, certain things might get a little... let's say, 'untidy'. It's only natural. However, before you present your startup to potential investors, it's essential to be prepared for an intense level of scrutiny.

Start with your financials. These are the bones of your business, and investors will look at them closely. Are your accounts in order? Do your projections make sense? Are there any unexplained expenses or irregularities? Before anyone else looks at them, examine them yourself or with your CFO. Make sure you can confidently answer any questions that come your way. And if there are aspects of your financials that look questionable - address them head-on. Investors appreciate transparency, even if the truth is a bit uncomfortable.

Next, look at your team. One thing I've observed over the years is that investors don't just invest in ideas - they invest in people. Ensure that every team member, especially the leadership, has their credentials and achievements well-documented. It's not about bragging, it's about proving that your team has the chops to take this startup to the next level.

Then there's the product or service itself. Make sure that any claims you make can be substantiated. If you say your software can do something, be prepared to show it. If you claim a certain market share, back it up with data.

But here's the golden nugget: Embrace the scrutiny. Yes, you heard me right. It's like a rigorous workout – it might be tough, but it makes you stronger. The process of preparing for investor scrutiny will help you tighten your ship, address any lingering issues, and emerge with a better, more resilient business.

Always remember, it's not about being perfect; it's about being real. Authenticity and transparency are your allies. They show potential investors that you're genuine, trustworthy, and prepared to tackle challenges head-on. And when that sunlight shines on your business, let it reveal a venture that's robust, honest, and ready to soar.

Overcoming Potential Red Flags

As an entrepreneur, I've faced my share of setbacks. There's no escaping them; it's the nature of the startup beast. But let's face it, some setbacks resonate louder than others, especially in the ears of potential investors. They see them as red flags—warnings that perhaps your venture isn't the golden goose they're searching for. But here's the thing about red flags: they aren't death sentences. They're challenges, and if there's one thing a founder knows, it's how to face challenges head-on.

Every startup has its own narrative. Some tales are of rapid growth and success, while others involve overcoming incredible odds. Often, it's those very odds, the red flags, that shape and refine us. They make our narratives rich, compelling, and ultimately, relatable.

For instance, perhaps your initial product launch wasn't the roaring success you'd hoped for. Maybe it was even a failure. While on the surface, this might seem like a major red flag, it's also an opportunity. Why? Because you learned from it. You took feedback, refined your product, and came back stronger. Share that journey. Investors often look beyond the stumble and focus on the recovery.

Or maybe your red flag is personnel-related. Did a co-founder leave abruptly? While this might raise eyebrows, it's your response that truly matters. How did you rally the team? What steps did you take to ensure stability? Demonstrating resilience and adaptability in the face of such challenges can be more convincing than a smooth-sailing journey.

Financial inconsistencies are another common concern. If your startup faced a particularly lean quarter, or if there was an investment that didn't quite pan out, address it head-on. Talk about the lessons learned, the measures implemented to prevent similar issues, and the strategies you have in place moving forward.

At the end of the day, remember this: Investors aren't just looking for perfection. They're looking for grit, resilience, adaptability, and a commitment to growth. They want to see founders who don't fold at the first sign of trouble but instead dig in their heels, learn, and come back even stronger.

So, when those red flags flutter, don't be disheartened. Embrace them. Use them as badges of your journey, testament to your resilience, and proof that no matter what comes your way, you're built to overcome. Because in the world of startups, it's not the absence of challenges that defines us, but how we rise above them.

10. **Negotiation Tactics and Strategies**

The Art of the Deal

In the rich tapestry of an entrepreneur's journey, one of the most exhilarating, yet nerve-wracking chapters is the pursuit of funding. At its core, fundraising is more than just a transaction; it's the bridge that links dreams to reality, ideas to execution. But herein lies the art: How do you, a passionate founder with a dream nestled close to your heart, convince someone to invest not just in your product but in you?

Imagine this moment: Across a polished table sits someone who could potentially unlock the next phase of your startup's growth. This isn't a simple pitch; it's a story, a narrative that weaves together your past struggles, present achievements, and future aspirations. You're not just asking for funds; you're inviting them into a shared dream.

One of the subtleties in this dance of fundraising is understanding that investors aren't merely looking for a return on investment. They're searching for founders who radiate passion, resilience, and vision. They want to believe, just as fervently as you do, in the transformative power of your startup. Your job, then, is not merely to present facts and figures, but to tell a story that resonates, that stirs something deep within, compelling them to join your journey.

As you traverse this landscape, bear in mind that every investor interaction is a two-way street. It's not just about them believing in you, but also about you assessing if they're the right fit for your company's ethos and culture. Do they share your values? Do they understand your mission? The right investor can be an invaluable ally, offering guidance, mentorship, and connections, far beyond the capital they bring.

However, with the highs come the lows. Rejections are an inevitable part of the fundraising saga. But here's the silver lining: Every 'no' brings you closer to that resounding 'yes'. It's crucial to remember that not every deal, no matter how glittering on paper, aligns with your startup's heart and soul. Sometimes, the most empowering decision is to gracefully decline and move forward.

In the end, the art of the fundraising deal is a delicate dance of conviction, resilience, and authenticity. It's about standing at the crossroads of dreams and reality and daring to believe that your vision is worth every ounce of effort. So, dear founders, as you step onto this stage, may you dance with both passion and grace, forging partnerships that propel your startup to unimaginable heights.

Balancing Equity, Control, and Growth

In the world of startups, there's an intricate dance every founder must master: the balancing act between equity, control, and growth. It's the crux of many sleepless nights, countless boardroom discussions, and reflections over that late-night cup of coffee. As a founder, you're constantly juggling the dreams you harbor for your brainchild and the very real constraints of the entrepreneurial world.

Let's take a moment to break this down. Equity is more than just a percentage on paper. It's a reflection of your blood, sweat, tears, and countless hours poured into your venture. And yet, to make your dream a tangible reality, there often comes a time when you need to part with a piece of that equity to bring in the resources, expertise, and partnerships that propel your startup to the next phase.

But here lies the rub. With equity often comes the relinquishing of some degree of control. Those shares you give away might mean a seat at the table for someone with a voice and a vision that might not always align with yours. The fear, of course, is that the startup you've nurtured from a mere idea might drift from its original course or ethos.

However, this dance isn't about compromise; it's about strategic growth. There's an empowering perspective to this: By sharing equity, you're not losing; you're gaining allies. Allies who believe in your vision enough to invest in it. Allies who bring a wealth of experience, insights, and networks that could be the catalyst for your startup's explosive growth.

Still, the key is balance. Understand what you're willing to give and what's non-negotiable for you. Reflect on what control means in the context of your startup's journey. Sometimes, maintaining 100% control can stifle growth, while at other times, relinquishing too much can derail your original vision. It's about finding that sweet spot where equity, control, and growth intersect to create a thriving, dynamic venture.

In your journey, dear founder, remember this: The road to success is paved with decisions that challenge us, push our boundaries, and demand introspection. Yet, at the heart of it all, it's about staying true to your vision while being open to the possibilities that come with collaboration and shared ownership.

As you navigate the challenging terrain of equity, control, and growth, may you find the wisdom to make decisions that honor both your startup's essence and its boundless potential. Your entrepreneurial dance is a testament to your resilience, passion, and vision. Embrace it, learn from it, and let it guide you to heights you've only dreamed of.

When to Walk Away

In the vibrant tapestry of the startup world, there's a thread that often goes unspoken: the moment a founder considers walking away. It's a poignant moment, filled with introspection, memories, and hopes for the future. Yet, it's a crucial crossroad that many founders will confront as they journey through the unpredictable terrain of entrepreneurship.

It's been said that startups are like babies to their founders. They're birthed from a mere idea, nurtured through sleepless nights, and raised amidst a mix of joyous milestones and challenging adversities. So, the very notion of walking away or taking a step back might seem unfathomable. And yet, it can be one of the most profound decisions a founder can make for the betterment of their creation.

You see, being a founder is an act of unparalleled passion and vision. But that very passion and vision can sometimes obscure an essential truth: the skills and temperament required to start a venture are not always the same as those needed to scale it. While a founder might excel at ideation, innovation, and initial execution, the expansive realm of management, strategy, and large-scale operations might call for a different kind of leadership.

It's a humbling realization but one steeped in strength and clarity. Recognizing when your startup might benefit from a different leadership style or expertise isn't an admission of inadequacy; it's a testament to your dedication to the venture's long-term success.

Consider this: a tree, when allowed to grow in its natural rhythm and direction, flourishes best. Similarly, there might come a point where, for your startup to truly soar, you need to entrust it to someone with the wings better suited for the next phase of the journey. It doesn't diminish your role or contribution; in fact, it magnifies it. It shows that your commitment to the startup's vision surpasses personal ambition.

To my fellow founders reading this, I implore you to always keep the bigger picture in mind. It's not about titles, ego, or legacy. It's about creating something that stands the test of time, impacts lives, and continues to innovate. If a moment comes when stepping aside or taking on a new role ensures that, embrace it with grace and the knowledge that your act is one of profound love and vision for your startup.

In the grand narrative of your entrepreneurial journey, remember that every decision, including when to walk away or step back, shapes the legacy of what you've built. Your heart, passion, and foresight will always be the cornerstone of your startup's success story.

11. **Post-Funding: Using Capital Wisely**

Managing Investor Relationships

In our journey as founders, we often view securing investment as the mountaintop — the culmination of countless pitches, negotiations, and sleepless nights. Yet, once the euphoria fades and the ink dries, a new expedition begins: managing investor relationships. This journey is less about the destination and more about the rhythm, trust, and understanding that unfolds between two partners.

Imagine being handed the keys to a classic, coveted car. It's pristine, powerful, and has immense potential. This car represents your startup. Now, imagine being told you need a co-driver, someone to navigate the treacherous turns and support the acceleration on open roads. This co-driver is your investor. The road trip you're embarking on together? It's the thrilling yet challenging path of turning a vision into a legacy.

As a founder, understanding that an investor is not merely a silent partner or a mere financier, but an active contributor to the journey is vital. They've placed trust in your vision, and in return, they seek not just monetary returns but a symbiotic relationship that's rooted in mutual respect, openness, and growth.

Here are a few guideposts to illuminate this journey:

1. **Open Communication:** Just as you'd update a friend about the highs and lows of your life, your investor deserves transparency. They've bet on you. Share with them not only the milestones but also the stumbling blocks. It fosters trust and often, they can provide insights or connections that could be pivotal.

2. **Active Listening:** It's easy to get defensive when someone critiques your 'baby', but remember, investors have a vantage point that you might not always see from the trenches. Their feedback, while sometimes hard to swallow, often comes from a place of wanting the best for the venture.

3. **Celebrate Together:** Every milestone, whether it's breaking even or launching a new product, is a testament to the combined efforts of the founder and the faith of the investor. Celebrate these moments, however small, to nurture the camaraderie.

4. **Set Boundaries:** While openness is crucial, it's also essential to set boundaries. A founder's role is to run the company, and while inputs from investors are invaluable, the final decision should often rest with the founder. Navigating this delicate balance is an art that gets refined with experience.

5. **Plan for the Long Haul:** Investor relationships aren't just for the duration of the funding cycle. They're long-term partnerships that can span various phases of your startup. Cultivate them with the same dedication and care you'd give to a lifelong friend.

Remember, fellow founders, the dance with your investors is a delicate one. It's filled with dips and twirls, highs and lows. Yet, when done right, it's a dance that can lead to an orchestra of success and innovation. Your vision lit the spark, but together with your investors, you'll fan the flames to create a blaze that lights up the entrepreneurial sky.

Scaling Your Business Responsibly

Ah, the siren call of scaling. It's a melody that beckons to every founder. That tantalizing dance between growth and sustainability, between rapid expansion and maintaining the very essence of what made your startup unique in the first place. As founders, the prospect of scaling is both exhilarating and, dare I say, a tad intimidating. But here's the golden nugget of wisdom I've gleaned from my years in the trenches: scaling, when done responsibly, can be the most rewarding phase of your entrepreneurial journey.

Scaling is not just about multiplying numbers or expanding to new territories. It's about growth that respects the core values of your business, that takes into consideration the well-being of your employees, and that remains committed to delivering value to your customers.

Think of your startup as a sapling. In its early days, it requires tender care, the right amount of sunlight, and protection from harsh elements. As it grows, its roots delve deeper, and its branches spread wider. But for it to become the majestic tree you envision, you must nurture it at every stage, ensuring it doesn't grow too wild or lose its essence.

Here's the thing: In the race to scale, it's easy to get caught up in the whirlwind of numbers and lose sight of the 'why' behind your startup. But remember, every decision to grow — whether it's hiring new talent, expanding product lines, or entering new markets — should resonate with the mission that set you on this path.

One of the most pivotal aspects of responsible scaling is understanding that growth should never come at the expense of quality. Whether it's the quality of your product, your team's work-life balance, or the relationship with your stakeholders, responsible scaling is about upholding these standards, even as you amplify your reach.

Another cornerstone is adaptability. As you scale, you'll encounter unforeseen challenges. The market dynamics might shift, or a global event might change the game. In these moments, clinging rigidly to a set plan can be more detrimental than beneficial. Adaptability allows you to pivot, reassess, and realign your growth strategies, ensuring that your scale remains rooted in relevance.

Lastly, surround yourself with a team that shares your vision of responsible growth. As a founder, your energy sets the tone, but it's the collective spirit of your team that carries the mission forward. When every member is aligned with the ethos of scaling responsibly, you create a symphony of coordinated effort that propels your startup to new heights, all while keeping its heart intact.

To my fellow founders, scaling is more than just a phase in your startup's journey. It's a testament to your vision, tenacity, and the impact you dream of creating in the world. As you stand on the precipice of this new adventure, remember to scale with intention, with respect for your roots, and with an unwavering commitment to the values that set you apart. In doing so, you won't just grow your business — you'll elevate it.

Preparing for the Next Funding Round: Charting the Path Forward with Clarity and Confidence

Ah, the exhilaration of a successful funding round! The late nights, the fervent pitches, the nail-biting waits, and then, the sweet, sweet victory. But here's the catch: in the dynamic world of startups, resting on laurels isn't an option. As one chapter closes, the preparation for the next beckons. And while the road to the subsequent funding round might seem daunting, with the right mindset and strategy, it can be as rewarding as the first.

Every time I've found myself at the crossroads of a new funding round, a quote by the legendary Wayne Gretzky comes to mind: "Skate to where the puck is going, not where it has been." As founders, our vision must be fixed on the future. The previous funding round was about where you were; the next is about where you intend to go.

First and foremost, understand that your narrative needs to evolve. While your initial story was about potential and promise, the sequel should showcase progress, milestones achieved, and a clearer roadmap for the future. Investors aren't just backing a vision; they're backing visible growth and a track record that inspires confidence.

One of the greatest lessons I've learned is the value of introspection. Before diving into the whirlpool of pitches and presentations, take a moment to reflect. Celebrate your successes, yes, but also critically assess areas of improvement. Were there commitments you couldn't meet? Were there unexpected hurdles? Transparency is not just about trust; it's about showcasing your ability to learn, adapt, and evolve.

It's also essential to re-familiarize yourself with the investment landscape. The ecosystem is ever-evolving, with new players, shifting priorities, and emerging trends. Your preparation should include a deep dive into understanding the current investment climate and how your startup fits into this larger tapestry.

Building on existing relationships is key. The rapport you've cultivated with your current investors can be an invaluable asset. Keep them in the loop, update them on progress, and engage them in your journey. Their insights, born from experience and vested interest, can offer perspectives you hadn't considered.

Lastly, remember that every funding round is a fresh opportunity to recommit to your mission. While the figures, forecasts, and strategies are crucial, the heart of your pitch remains the 'why' of your startup. Why does it matter? Why should it exist? And why, among a sea of options, is your venture worth believing in?

To my fellow founders gearing up for the next round, remember: fundraising is as much about conviction as it is about numbers. As you prepare to step into the arena once more, arm yourself with clarity, passion, and a vision that not only captivates but also compels. Because at the end of the day, it's not just about securing funds — it's about forging partnerships that fuel the journey ahead.

12. **Alternative Funding Options**

Chapter 12: Crowdfunding: Engaging the Masses

In a world brimming with ideas and potential, there's a rhythm to innovation that beckons us to march to its beat. Every founder has their tale, their fire, their dream that drives them. But sometimes, the conventional path to funding might not align with our stories or our unique visions. Enter crowdfunding—an avenue that is as much about connecting heartbeats as it is about connecting wallets.

Imagine having the chance not just to attract investors, but to cultivate a tribe — a community that resonates with your idea and is willing to pledge their hard-earned money, not for equity, but simply for the belief in a dream. That's the essence of crowdfunding.

Now, why would a startup founder like you or me tread this path? It's because crowdfunding is more than just about capital. It's a validation of your vision, a testament to its appeal, and a litmus test for its potential in the real world. It's grassroots, it's real, and most importantly, it's personal.

When I embarked on my crowdfunding journey, I was surprised by its depth. It wasn't just about putting up a product and asking for money. It was about crafting a narrative, engaging with backers, and nurturing a community spirit. I learned quickly that this was a two-way street; it's as much about giving as it is about receiving. Sharing regular updates, acknowledging feedback, celebrating milestones — all these became as pivotal as the funds pouring in.

Yet, the magic of crowdfunding doesn't come without its challenges. It demands transparency, relentless communication, and a genuine commitment to delivering on promises. It's a public stage, and setbacks are visible to all. But therein lies its power. Every challenge faced and overcome in the public eye becomes a story, a testimony to the resilience and dedication of a founder and their team.

For those considering this path, remember that crowdfunding is not an easier alternative to traditional fundraising — it's just different. It requires heart, authenticity, and a genuine desire to bring people along on your journey.

In essence, crowdfunding is the embodiment of a shared dream. It's where the boundaries between founder and supporter blur, and everyone becomes a stakeholder in a vision that promises to change the world, one pledge at a time. So, to all my fellow founders, I urge you to consider this path, not just as a means to an end, but as an experience that can enrich your startup journey in ways you'd never imagined.

Chapter 12: Grants and Competitions - The Unexpected Path to Funding

Starting up is an exhilarating journey, with each turn presenting a blend of opportunities and challenges. As founders, we're always on the lookout for fuel to propel our dreams further. While venture capital and angel investors often dominate the fundraising conversations, there are other avenues equally filled with potential: grants and competitions.

Ah, grants. These golden tickets. They're not just about the money (though that's undeniably great). Grants represent validation from organizations and institutions that see the potential in your vision. They're a nod of approval, a pat on the back, an affirmation that you're on to something special. And the best part? It's funding without dilution. This isn't equity you're parting with; it's a gift to help you soar.

Competitions, on the other hand, offer a stage. It's not just about winning, though the accolades and prizes can be transformative. It's about the process — the preparation, the pitch, the feedback. These contests sharpen our narrative, challenge our assumptions, and often introduce us to a network of mentors, peers, and investors. The adrenaline rush of standing on that stage, pouring your heart out, defending your idea, and then, the drumroll as the winners are announced — it's an experience every founder should cherish.

I've walked this path, friends. I've felt the nervous energy before presenting to a panel of seasoned judges, the late nights refining every word of a grant application, and the sheer joy of being recognized. But beyond the funds and accolades, these experiences honed my skills, expanded my network, and deepened my belief in our mission.

Yet, diving into this world requires a mindset shift. It's about embracing humility, being open to feedback, and recognizing that there's always something new to learn. Each application, each pitch, is an opportunity for introspection and growth.

To those considering this avenue, let me share a piece of advice: Don't just chase the money. Seek out grants and competitions that align with your values, your industry, and your vision. It's a journey of alignment. When you find the right fit, the journey is incredibly rewarding.

In the grand tapestry of startup fundraising, grants and competitions might seem like mere threads. But when woven together with passion, dedication, and purpose, they can add rich textures and patterns, making your startup story truly one for the ages.

Debt Financing and Loans

In the heart of the startup realm, where equity and venture capital often take center stage, there exists another, more traditional protagonist: Debt. For many, the word 'debt' may carry a certain weight, an echo of cautionary tales from the past. But in the hands of a strategic founder, debt can become a powerful tool, one that can provide the much-needed runway without relinquishing a piece of your dream.

Debt financing, at its core, is about belief. It's a belief in your vision, in your team, and, most importantly, in your ability to generate returns. While equity financing can sometimes feel like a pact, where you're giving away a part of your baby, debt is more like a trust exercise. It's the financial world saying, "We believe you can scale these heights, and we're giving you a boost."

Loans and lines of credit are not mere transactions; they're partnerships with financial institutions. They require discipline, meticulous planning, and a deep understanding of your business's financial health. Yes, there's interest to be paid, and yes, there's a commitment to repay. But these are not burdens; they're badges of trust, markers of mutual respect between you and your lender.

In my own journey, I've felt the empowerment that comes from securing a business loan. The moment you see those funds hit your account, it's not just capital you've gained; it's confidence. It's a testament to the solidity of your business plan, to the potential seen by outsiders, and to the future revenue you're poised to generate.

However, it's paramount to approach debt financing with clear eyes and a strategic mindset. It's not a one-size-fits-all solution. For some startups, especially those with long lead times to profitability, equity might be a better fit. But for others, especially those with tangible assets, predictable revenue streams, or those looking to finance a specific project, debt can be an excellent ally.

Embracing debt is like mastering an art. It demands a delicate balance, a dance between ambition and caution. It's about leveraging the present for a brighter, self-sustained future. And when navigated with wisdom, it allows you to retain ownership and control, ensuring that your vision remains undiluted and true to its origins.

In the entrepreneurial symphony, debt financing is a subtle yet potent instrument. It can complement your equity arrangements, provide flexibility, and offer a vote of confidence in your venture. After all, in this world of innovation and disruption, sometimes the old ways, when wielded with creativity and purpose, can lead to the most profound breakthroughs.

13. **Challenges and Setbacks**

Common Roadblocks in Fundraising

Every founder's journey is laden with its own set of challenges, but when it comes to fundraising, many of us share common threads. These roadblocks, while daunting, are not insurmountable. In fact, they can become stepping stones, teaching us invaluable lessons about our businesses and ourselves.

Starting a business is akin to lighting a torch in the darkness. That initial spark is your idea, your vision. However, as you tread this entrepreneurial path, seeking funds to fuel your vision, gusts of wind, in the form of obstacles, threaten to extinguish your flame. Recognizing these gusts early can be the difference between a faltering flame and a raging bonfire.

One of the most common challenges is the 'Mismatched Vision'. You may have had those meetings where, despite your passionate pitch, the investor just doesn't share your enthusiasm. Remember, not every investor will resonate with your idea, and that's okay. It's essential to find those who truly believe in your vision and align with your company's core values.

Then there's the 'Unmet Milestones' challenge. Perhaps you promised a certain traction level by quarter three, but external factors put you behind schedule. These moments test your resilience and adaptability. They push you to communicate, to reset expectations, and to demonstrate your commitment to navigating rough waters.

'Market Skepticism' is another frequent visitor in our fundraising adventures. Sometimes, the world isn't ready for our innovations, or perhaps, they just don't see the potential we do. Convincing investors requires a blend of hard data, a compelling narrative, and an unyielding belief in what you're building.

But amidst these challenges, the most profound roadblock can sometimes be our own 'Self-Doubt'. The fundraising journey, with its highs and lows, can lead us to question our worth and the viability of our dreams. It's during these moments that we must remember why we started, lean on our support systems, and trust in our vision's transformative power.

Overcoming these roadblocks isn't about sidestepping them or seeking shortcuts. It's about facing them head-on, armed with research, preparedness, and genuine passion. Each obstacle, while frustrating in its immediacy, offers an opportunity for growth, refinement, and clarity.

In my entrepreneurial voyage, I've come to see these challenges not as deterrents but as essential chapters in a riveting tale of ambition, perseverance, and triumph. They have shaped me, guided me, and most importantly, taught me that the journey, with all its hurdles, is as valuable as the destination.

To my fellow founders, as you navigate your fundraising path, remember that every great endeavor faces resistance. Embrace these roadblocks, learn from them, and let them propel you forward. For in the end, it's not the absence of challenges but the spirit with which we face them that defines our entrepreneurial legacy.

Bouncing Back from Rejection'

Ah, rejection. That uninvited guest we've all met at some point in our entrepreneurial journey. It stings, doesn't it? When you've poured heart and soul into your startup, hearing a 'no' from an investor can feel like a personal affront. But, dear founder, rejection, as I've come to understand it, is not an endpoint but rather a detour to a potentially better destination.

If there's one universal truth in the world of startups, it's this: every founder will hear 'no' more times than they'd like. Yet, it's the founders who learn to interpret and bounce back from these rejections that carve their path to success.

Imagine, for a moment, that every rejection is a mirror. It reflects back not a failure, but an opportunity to reflect, refine, and recalibrate. Every 'no' holds a lesson – perhaps it's about the market fit, maybe the financial projections, or even the storytelling aspect of your pitch.

The first step in bouncing back is understanding that rejection is rarely absolute. Investors have a myriad of reasons to decline - sometimes it's about their fund's strategy, their current portfolio mix, or even the stage your company is at. It's not always about you or your idea.

Next, seek feedback. This can be a gold mine. Constructive criticism illuminates areas of improvement and offers insights that you might have missed in your entrepreneurial fervor. Embrace it, act on it, and let it guide your next steps.

Now, here's the part where your resilience truly shines: the comeback. Armed with feedback, rework your strategy, sharpen your pitch, and approach the next investor with renewed vigor. Remember, every successful founder has a story filled with rejections, but it's their unwavering spirit and adaptability that we celebrate.

Rejection also serves as a litmus test for your passion. If you can weather the storm of multiple 'nos' and still wake up burning with the same drive, it's a testament to your commitment. And this relentless spirit is precisely what investors ultimately seek.

In my journey, I've faced my share of closed doors. But looking back, I realize they steered me towards better fits, fresh perspectives, and unforeseen opportunities. Rejection, in its own peculiar way, refined my mission and deepened my resolve.

To all my fellow founders, remember that every 'no' brings you one step closer to that resounding 'yes'. In the vast tapestry of your entrepreneurial story, these rejections will be mere stitches, holding together the larger, beautiful narrative of your success. Embrace them, learn from them, and let them propel you into the future you're tirelessly working towards.

Navigating Changes in Market Conditions

The entrepreneurial journey, much like sailing, is never a straight path from point A to point B. Instead, it's an odyssey, filled with serene stretches of calm and sudden, unexpected storms. Changes in market conditions are those unpredictable gusts of wind that can either capsize your boat or propel you forward with newfound momentum.

As a founder, I've seen the ebbs and flows, the booms and busts, and I can tell you firsthand: the market's whims are not for the faint-hearted. But for those willing to adjust their sails, to learn and adapt, these changes can present unforeseen opportunities.

First and foremost, it's vital to remember that market conditions are external; they're beyond our control. But our response? That's entirely up to us. In times of market upheaval, our vision, adaptability, and resilience are tested. These are the moments where true entrepreneurial spirit shines.

One lesson I've cherished is the value of agility. Staying attuned to market shifts, and more importantly, being willing to pivot or refine your strategy, is paramount. This agility, coupled with a deep understanding of your core value proposition, can be your guiding star. Even if the whole world seems to be shifting underfoot, knowing your essence allows you to move and adapt without losing sight of who you are and what your startup stands for.

Another invaluable asset during tumultuous market conditions? Your team. Surrounding yourself with a diverse group of thinkers ensures that you have multiple perspectives to draw upon. When the market zigs, a varied team can help you decide whether to zag or to zig along in a way that's still true to your startup's mission.

And let's not forget the value of relationships, especially with those who've been through these storms before. Fellow founders, mentors, even competitors, can provide insights, share strategies, and often, simply empathize. There's a collective wisdom in the entrepreneurial community, a reservoir of knowledge built from countless trials by fire. Tap into it.

In the end, while market shifts are inevitable, they are also temporary. With a clear vision, a willingness to adapt, and the support of a robust community, you can not only navigate these changes but harness them to drive your startup to new heights. As the saying goes, "A smooth sea never made a skilled sailor." Embrace the waves, adjust your sails, and let the winds of change guide you towards uncharted territories and unimaginable success.

14. **Case Studies: Success Stories and Cautionary Tales**

Startup A: From Garage to Global Phenomenon

As the evening sun cast long, dappled shadows across a small suburban garage, a spark of innovation was kindled. Amidst the clutter of old family keepsakes and half-finished projects, 'Startup A' was born. It was a humble beginning for a venture that would one day command the attention of the world, but as every founder knows, true innovation doesn't require a polished boardroom—it only needs passion, determination, and a vision.

It's not the grandeur of where you begin, but the magnitude of your vision and the vigor of your pursuit that defines your journey. Startup A's inception was far from glamorous, but its founders saw a gap in the market that no one else did. Armed with little more than a prototype, they embarked on an adventure that would be punctuated with challenges and celebrated with triumphs.

While they had an innovative product, they understood the importance of effective fundraising. They recognized that having a good idea was just the beginning. To scale it, to take it to the masses, and to make it a global phenomenon, they needed the right resources. They would soon enter the world of pitching, negotiating, and partnership-building.

The first pitch didn't go as planned. Investors raised eyebrows, skeptically mulling over the product's potential. But instead of being disheartened, the team used each rejection as a stepping stone. They refined their pitch, understood the market better, and came back stronger. When one door closed, they knocked on two more.

Their perseverance paid off. One day, they walked into a room, and the chemistry was instant. The investors saw not just a product, but a vision, a team, and the burning passion to make it all come true. They secured their first significant investment, and with that, the gears of Startup A shifted into rapid motion.

But even as they scaled, they faced challenges, ones they hadn't anticipated. Market shifts, copycat competitors, internal disagreements—yet through it all, their initial spark, that magic from the garage days, never dimmed. It was this unwavering spirit that saw them through, turning naysayers into advocates and challenges into opportunities.

In the end, Startup A wasn't just about a product or even its founders. It was a testament to the spirit of innovation, the importance of resilience, and the magic that happens when you refuse to give up, no matter the odds.

Founders, as you embark on your journey, remember the story of Startup A. Not every day will be easy, but every challenge is an opportunity in disguise. Hold onto your vision, believe in your journey, and know that from humble beginnings, global phenomena can indeed arise.

Startup B: A Bumpy Ride to Acquisition

Beneath the gleaming lights of a city that never sleeps, three ambitious souls huddled together in a dimly lit café. Their conversation? The inception of 'Startup B'. This wasn't just a business to them; it was a dream—a dream they were willing to chase down every alleyway and avenue.

Startup B's journey wasn't characterized by the meteoric rises you often hear about. Instead, it was defined by resilience, adaptability, and an uncanny ability to find silver linings in even the most challenging situations. They began with a unique product—a solution to a problem many didn't even realize existed.

The early days were marked by intense excitement. Initial user feedback was promising, and the small team grew with every ounce of positive reinforcement. However, as they expanded, so did the number of obstacles they encountered.

Market fluctuations made their revenue model volatile. Hiring missteps led to a disjointed company culture. Negative press from one poor decision threatened to overshadow their years of hard work. Each challenge felt like a pothole, jolting them off their course. Yet, with each bump in the road, they refined their approach and learned invaluable lessons about the landscape of the startup world.

Fundraising was its own beast. The founders navigated countless meetings with potential investors — some encouraging, others disheartening. They faced rejection, skepticism, and even mockery. Yet, every 'no' only reinforced their commitment to the 'yes' they believed was just around the corner.

And then, it happened. A strategic partner saw the potential in merging Startup B's unique offerings with their established platform. Acquisition talks began. It wasn't a straightforward process — there were negotiations, sleepless nights, and moments when it felt like the deal would fall through.

But, as with every other challenge they'd faced, the team of Startup B met the acquisition process with determination and tenacity. They knew their worth, they understood the value they could bring to the table, and they weren't willing to settle for anything less than what they deserved.

When the ink finally dried on the acquisition papers, it marked the end of one journey and the beginning of another. Startup B had weathered the storm, proving that success isn't just about the destination — it's about the journey and the lessons learned along the way.

To all founders reading this: your path might not be smooth, but that's okay. The bumps, detours, and unexpected twists? They shape you, refine your vision, and prepare you for the opportunities you can't even see yet. Embrace the ride, for it's in the challenges that the real stories of success are forged.

Startup C: Lessons from a Failed Fundraising Attempt

Startup C's tale is not a triumphant one, at least not in the traditional sense. Yet, it's a story that every founder should hear, for it encapsulates the harsh realities, invaluable lessons, and the unyielding spirit that defines the entrepreneurial journey.

From the outside looking in, Startup C had all the markers of a rising star. An innovative product, a dedicated team, and a market that seemed ripe for disruption. As they dove headfirst into fundraising, the air was thick with hope and ambition. Each pitch was delivered with passion, each meeting entered with optimism. But as weeks turned into months, that initial enthusiasm began to wane. The anticipated offers of funding were not materializing.

It wasn't that they didn't have meetings; they did. Many of them. But they were met with a mix of lukewarm responses and polite declines. Feedback was varied and at times contradictory. One investor felt the market was too niche, another thought it too broad. Some wanted a pivot in product direction, while others felt the original vision was lost.

Disappointment set in, but so did introspection. The founders of Startup C began to peel back the layers, seeking to understand where they might have gone astray. They realized that while their vision was clear, their story wasn't. The narrative they presented to investors lacked cohesion and failed to address potential concerns preemptively.

In this introspection, they also discovered that they had perhaps been too eager to please, too willing to adapt to each piece of feedback without critically evaluating its merit. In trying to be everything to every potential investor, they had lost the essence of what made Startup C unique.

But failure, as they say, is the best teacher. The experience, as bitter as it was, offered clarity. The team regrouped, refocused, and embarked on a journey to refine their offering and narrative. They learned the importance of authenticity, of staying true to one's vision while being open to genuine feedback. They understood that not every investor is the right fit, and that's okay.

Startup C's fundraising journey didn't yield the desired funds, but it gifted them something equally valuable – perspective. Today, they stand stronger, wiser, and more prepared for the challenges of the entrepreneurial world.

For all founders out there, Startup C's story is a testament to the idea that setbacks are but stepping stones. Fundraising is as much about understanding oneself as it is about understanding the market. And sometimes, the lessons learned from the journeys that don't go as planned are the ones that truly set you up for future success.

15. **Conclusion: The Road Ahead**

Embracing the Journey of Entrepreneurship

Ah, entrepreneurship! It's a word that encapsulates dreams, ambitions, challenges, and yes, even failures. But to me, and probably to many of you reading this, it's a word that signifies hope. It's a testament to human spirit, to our boundless capacity to imagine and then strive to make those imaginations come to life. Whether you're at the beginning of your startup journey, or you're several rounds deep into fundraising, this chapter is an ode to that spirit, to the entrepreneur in each one of us.

When I embarked on my entrepreneurial path, I was fueled by an intense passion for my idea, and a belief that it could change the world. And I'm sure it's the same for many of you. This burning desire to innovate, to disrupt, and to make a difference is what keeps us going, even in the face of seemingly insurmountable challenges.

Yet, as we delve deeper into the world of startups and fundraising, we also come to realize that this journey is as much about personal growth as it is about business growth. We learn to navigate the highs and lows, to celebrate the victories, no matter how small, and to embrace the lessons that come from our setbacks. We understand the true value of resilience, tenacity, and adaptability.

Fundraising, especially, is a whirlwind. It's a dance of numbers, projections, negotiations, and, very importantly, human connections. It teaches us humility, as we put our dreams in front of others and ask them to believe in us. It teaches us grit, as we push forward, despite the rejections and the naysayers. And most crucially, it teaches us the importance of authenticity, of staying true to our vision and values, even as we adapt to the ever-changing landscapes of business.

I've often been asked what the secret sauce is to successful fundraising or building a thriving startup. While there's no one-size-fits-all answer, I believe it's a blend of unwavering belief in your idea, the ability to adapt and learn, and the courage to stay the course, even when the going gets tough.

But above all, it's important to remember why we started on this path in the first place. It's that spark, that desire to bring something new into the world, to solve a problem, to touch lives. That, dear founders, is the essence of entrepreneurship. It's not just about the end goal, the exits, or the valuation. It's about the journey, the growth, the myriad experiences, and the memories we create along the way.

So, as you turn the pages of this book, and as you move forward on your own entrepreneurial path, I hope you remember to embrace every moment of this journey. Cherish the lessons, celebrate the milestones, and most importantly, believe in yourself and your vision. Because at the end of the day, that's what entrepreneurship is all about. It's a journey of faith, of dreams, and of endless possibilities. Embrace it with all your heart.

Continuing to Innovate and Grow

Every founder's journey is sprinkled with those rare "eureka!" moments. Moments when an idea seems to leap out of the cosmos and directly into our minds, setting our worlds aflame with potential. But, as we progress, many of us find that it's not just about that initial spark. It's about continuously fanning the flames, ensuring that the fire of innovation keeps burning brightly, guiding our startup to new heights.

In the world of startups, standing still is akin to moving backward. The pace of change is blistering, and the market is merciless to those who become complacent. Yes, you might have raised that first round of funding or launched that breakthrough product. Celebrate those wins, absolutely! But then, roll up your sleeves and dive back into the ocean of innovation, because that's where the real magic happens.

In my own entrepreneurial journey, I've often found inspiration in the unlikeliest of places. From a casual conversation at a café to an article in a magazine I picked up on a flight, ideas and possibilities are everywhere. Our task is to remain receptive, to keep our minds open, and to be brave enough to explore new avenues even when the old ones seem so comfortable.

One might think that once you've tasted success, once you've made that groundbreaking innovation, the pressure eases. In some ways, it does. But in many ways, it transforms. Now, you're not just tasked with proving your worth; you're tasked with outdoing yourself. It's a thrilling challenge, one that demands resilience, creativity, and a touch of madness.

And while we're on the topic of growth, let's not forget personal growth. As founders, we are, in many ways, the heartbeat of our startups. As we evolve, learn, and expand our horizons, so too does our business. Investing in ourselves, whether it's through continuous learning, networking, or simply taking breaks to rejuvenate, can often be the catalyst for our company's next big leap.

Remember, every great tree was once a tiny seedling. It didn't just sprout overnight. It faced storms, droughts, and countless challenges. Yet, it continued to grow, to reach for the skies, to expand its canopy. Our startups are much the same. There will be challenges, there will be naysayers, and there will be times when the path ahead seems obscured. But with continuous innovation, with a relentless drive to grow, and with a heart full of passion, the possibilities are endless.

In this ever-evolving dance of entrepreneurship, let innovation be your constant partner. Let growth, both personal and professional, be your North Star. And as you continue to scale new heights, remember to enjoy the view, for it's a testament to your hard work, your vision, and your unyielding spirit. Keep growing, keep innovating, and let your startup story inspire a whole new generation of dreamers.

16. **Appendices**
** Perfect Pitch Deck**

The first time I stood in front of potential investors, my heart was pounding so loudly I thought the entire room could hear it. I had spent countless hours preparing what I believed was the perfect presentation. In my hand, I clutched a remote that controlled the slides of what would become the most influential tool I'd ever created: my pitch deck. It wasn't just a collection of slides; it was the story of my dream, my passion, and the future I envisioned.

When we talk about pitch decks, many of us often picture flashy graphics, tons of data, and perhaps some buzzwords thrown in for good measure. But, in reality, a pitch deck is so much more than that. It's an entrepreneur's passport to the world of opportunities, the key to unlocking doors that seemed forever shut. It's the culmination of sleepless nights, rigorous brainstorming sessions, and that burning desire to make a mark in the world.

If you're reading this, you're likely on the brink of stepping into a world brimming with potential. You have an idea, a vision, and now you're seeking the fuel to turn that spark into a blazing trail. The pitch deck is your torch.

But let's demystify something right away: there's no one-size-fits-all approach. The "perfect pitch deck" isn't a universal template that every founder can download, fill in the blanks, and then magically secure funding. It's not about fitting into a mold; it's about breaking it. It's about showcasing your unique journey, your challenges, your triumphs, and your unwavering spirit.

The pages that follow won't give you a generic checklist. Instead, they'll guide you on how to weave your narrative, how to speak to the heart and the mind, and how to make those precious minutes in front of potential investors count. Remember, investors aren't just investing in an idea; they're investing in you, your team, and the world you're trying to shape.

So, take a deep breath, dear founder. Embark on this journey with an open heart and an eager mind. Let's craft not just a pitch deck, but a masterpiece that resonates, inspires, and most importantly, gets you one step closer to making your dream a tangible reality. Welcome to the art and soul of creating the perfect pitch deck.

1. **Introduction Slide**:
   - Name of the startup.
   - Tagline or brief descriptor.

2. **Problem Statement**:
   - Clearly define the problem you're addressing.
   - Use relatable examples or anecdotes.

3. **Solution**:
   - Introduce your product or service as the solution.
   - Highlight its unique selling proposition (USP).

4. **Product Demo/Service Walkthrough**:
   - Screenshots, diagrams, or even a short video of your product in action.

5. **Market Opportunity**:
   - Size of the target market.
   - Growth rate.
   - Potential market share capture.

6. **Business Model**:
   - How you plan to make money.
   - Details on pricing, distribution, and any recurring revenue.

7. **Go-to-Market Strategy**:
   - How you plan to acquire your first customers and expand.
   - Details about marketing and sales strategies.

8. **Traction**:
   - Customer testimonials, user metrics, or sales figures.
   - Graphs or charts showing growth or progress to date.

9. **Competitive Landscape**:

- Overview of key competitors and their positioning.
- What differentiates you from them.

10. **Financial Projections**:
  - Revenue, profit, and key metrics projections for the next 3-5 years.
  - Use charts for clear visualization.

11. **Ask**:
  - Clearly specify what you're asking from investors.
  - This can be funding amount, partnerships, or other resources.

12. **Team**:
  - Highlight key team members, their roles, and previous successes or relevant experience.

13. **Closing/Thank You Slide**:
  - Contact details.
  - Call-to-action, like scheduling a follow-up or demo.

Tips:

- **Keep it Concise**: The best pitch decks are clear and concise, aiming for 15-20 slides at most.

- **Visual Emphasis**: Use visuals (charts, images, infographics) to break up the text and drive your points home. This makes slides memorable and engaging.

- **Consistency**: Maintain a consistent theme throughout the pitch deck in terms of colors, fonts, and style.

- **Narrative Flow**: Your pitch deck should tell a story, moving seamlessly from identifying the problem to showcasing your solution, the opportunity, and why your team is the right one to tackle it.

- **Practice**: A pitch deck is only as good as the presentation itself. Practice your pitch so you can present each slide confidently and answer questions when they arise.

Remember, while this is a template, you should customize it according to the specific needs and strengths of your startup. Your pitch deck is a reflection of your business, so ensure it is polished, professional, and truly represents what you offer.

Glossary of Key Terms

In the world of startups and fundraising, it's easy to feel like you're wandering in a maze, surrounded by jargon and terms that sound foreign. But you're not alone. I recall the first board meeting I attended, nodding along to phrases I didn't fully understand, feeling like an impostor in a world I had passionately chosen. Over time, and after many whispered questions to colleagues and late-night Google searches, I got a handle on this intricate lingo.

Understanding these terms isn't about impressing investors with your fluency in "startup speak." It's about empowering you to navigate the intricacies of fundraising and scaling with confidence. So, as a fellow founder, I've put together this glossary to provide clarity and instill a sense of confidence as you venture into conversations, meetings, and negotiations.

- **Angel Investor:** Often, an individual who provides capital to startups in exchange for convertible debt or ownership equity. They're like the guardian angels of the startup world, guiding and supporting young companies.

- **Burn Rate:** The rate at which a company is spending its capital to run day-to-day operations. Think of it as the speedometer of your startup's financial health.

- **Convertible Note:** A short-term debt that converts into equity in the future, typically during a future funding round.

- **Due Diligence:** An extensive analysis investors conduct before committing capital to a startup. It's their way of peeking under the hood, ensuring everything's in order.

- **Equity:** Ownership interest in the startup. When investors talk about taking equity, they're referring to a piece of your company pie.

- **Liquidity Event:** A milestone where founders, investors, and other stakeholders can cash out their share, typically through a merger, acquisition, or IPO.

- **MVP (Minimum Viable Product):** The most basic version of your product that allows you to start the learning process as quickly as possible.

- **Term Sheet:** An agreement that outlines the major aspects of an investment. It's like a prenup for your startup and its investors.

- **Valuation:** The monetary value assigned to your startup. It's more art than science, blending cold hard numbers with the warmth of potential and promise.

- **Vesting:** A system where an employee's rights to company stock or benefits become the employee's over time. It's a mechanism to ensure long-term commitment.

While these terms may seem intimidating at first glance, they're just the tip of the iceberg. As you delve deeper into the startup ecosystem, you'll encounter many more. Embrace them. Seek to understand, not just memorize. And remember, it's okay to ask questions. Every founder, even the most seasoned among us, started somewhere.

Let this glossary be your guiding light, a beacon as you sail through the often stormy waters of entrepreneurship. With knowledge in your arsenal, you're well-equipped to forge meaningful connections, make informed decisions, and lead your venture towards unparalleled success.

Recommended Resources and Further Reading

Navigating the tumultuous waters of the startup ecosystem can feel overwhelming. But just as sailors once relied on stars to find their way across vast oceans, today's entrepreneurs have a wealth of resources to guide them. Over my years as a founder, I've found solace, guidance, and inspiration from a myriad of books, podcasts, and online platforms. And now, it's my pleasure to pass on these compass points to you. Let them light your path, just as they've illuminated mine.

Books:
- *Zero to One* by Peter Thiel: A thought-provoking dive into startups and how to build the future. It challenges the norms and urges entrepreneurs to think differently.

- *The Lean Startup* by Eric Ries: This book is foundational. It introduces the concept of lean methodology in startups, emphasizing agility and adaptability.

- *Venture Deals: Be Smarter Than Your Lawyer and Venture Capitalist* by Brad Feld and Jason Mendelson: A must-read if you're diving into the complex world of VC funding. It breaks down the nitty-gritty of deals in an accessible manner.

- *The Hard Thing About Hard Things* by Ben Horowitz: A raw, genuine look at the trials and tribulations of entrepreneurial life. Horowitz shares lessons from his own experiences, offering both cautionary tales and stories of hope.

Podcasts:
- *How I Built This with Guy Raz*: Real stories from the founders behind some of the world's best-known companies. It's an intimate look at the ups, downs, and turning points in their journeys.

- *The Pitch*: Think of it as Shark Tank in podcast form. Real entrepreneurs pitch to real investors—for real money.

- *Masters of Scale* hosted by Reid Hoffman: This podcast, by one of LinkedIn's co-founders, explores how companies grow from zero to a gazillion and the challenges they face along the way.

Online Platforms and Websites:
- *AngelList*: A platform for startups to meet investors, apply for funding, and post or apply for jobs.

- *Crunchbase*: A database of company, investor, and industry information. It's a fantastic place to research potential investors or competitors.

- *Y Combinator's Startup School*: An invaluable resource, offering a free online course for founders. It covers everything from product development to hiring to, of course, fundraising.

Every resource I've listed above has, at some point, provided me with insight, comfort, or the push I needed to make a challenging decision. Books offer the wisdom of those who've tread the path before us; podcasts provide real-time insights and relatable tales of success and failure, and online platforms connect us to a broader community, ensuring we never feel alone in our entrepreneurial journey.

Remember, the journey of a startup founder is as much about continuous learning as it is about innovation. Embrace every opportunity to grow, not just in business acumen but also in spirit and perspective. These resources are just the beginning. Your curiosity, drive, and passion will lead you to countless more. Happy reading and listening!

Chapter 17: Acknowledgments

When you're in the thick of building something from scratch, the days blur into nights, and it sometimes feels like you're climbing a mountain with no peak in sight. During these moments, it's the unwavering support of those around you that makes every challenge surmountable. This journey, while personal to each founder, is seldom embarked upon alone. As I pause to reflect on the winding road that has brought me to where I stand today, I'm filled with profound gratitude for every hand that held mine along the way.

First and foremost, I want to thank my co-founders. We've experienced the highs and lows together, celebrated wins, and picked up the pieces after setbacks. Our bond has only grown stronger with each hurdle we've faced, and I am endlessly thankful for the trust, resilience, and camaraderie we've shared.

To my family, your belief in me has been the bedrock on which I've built everything. Even during times when I couldn't articulate the vision that drove me, you stood by my side, cheering me on, offering wisdom, and sometimes, just lending a patient ear. Your unwavering faith and love have been the silent wind beneath my wings.

To our early investors and mentors, thank you for seeing potential in a nascent idea and a scrappy team. Your guidance, more than the funds, has been instrumental. You've been our lighthouses, guiding us away from potential pitfalls and towards opportunities we hadn't even envisioned.

A special mention to the countless entrepreneurs who've walked this path before me. Your stories of tenacity, grit, and ingenuity have been a constant source of inspiration. Every shared experience, every lesson learned the hard way, and every nugget of wisdom has been a beacon, illuminating the path for those of us who follow.

To the team that worked tirelessly on this book, especially my editor, who patiently sifted through endless drafts and shaped this work into its final form. Your passion and dedication mirror the very spirit this book aims to capture.

Lastly, to you, the reader and fellow founder, thank you for embarking on this journey with me. It's my sincere hope that this book provides you with clarity, insight, and, above all, the affirmation that you're not alone in this. Every founder's journey is unique, but we're all united in our passion, determination, and the unwavering belief in our dreams.

In this grand tapestry of entrepreneurship, every thread has its significance. Each one of you has been instrumental in weaving the story that I am so privileged to share today. From the depths of my heart, thank you.

Chapter 18: About the Author

Chapter 18: About the Author

In the vast tapestry of the entrepreneurial realm, Max Sea's journey stands as a testament to passion, resilience, and an unyielding commitment to innovation. When readers delve into this book, they are not merely absorbing wisdom; they are tracing the footprints of Max's two-decade-long adventure through the challenging yet rewarding world of startups.

Two decades ago, Max was a fervent university student, his mind bursting with innovative ideas. Little did the world know that this budding entrepreneur would go on to transform one of those ideas into a company that, merely three years later, would mark his first successful exit.

The journey wasn't always smooth. While Max saw four significant exits, one of which made waves in the digital content publishing space, he also faced his fair share of obstacles. But, Max's story is not just about the dazzling success of raising over 300 million dollars from a diverse pool of angels, crowdfunders, and venture capitalists. It's also a tale of perseverance. There were failures, but as Max often emphasizes, "If you don't try, you neither win nor fail."

Max's written legacy extends beyond the realm of startups. He's penned six books, each echoing his profound insights and experiences. After a remarkable exit in 2012, wherein he sold a company for a staggering $100 million, Max took a sabbatical. This break wasn't about resting on his laurels. Instead, he invested in 41 seed companies. The outcome? Only seven write-offs and four triumphant exits. This sabbatical served as a reflective period for Max, during which he realized his true calling wasn't just in investing. His heart yearned for the thrill of creation, the pulse of teamwork, and the intricate dance of executing ideas into realities.

Max has always been enamored with technology's potential, but not just for the sake of innovation. His vision is anchored in a profound desire to leverage technology to uplift and enhance the human experience.

Max Sea's legacy is not just about the businesses he built or the investments he made. It's a story of a man who, with unwavering determination and a passion for technology, dedicated his life to making a genuine impact. In this book, Max hopes to pass on the torch, inspiring and guiding the next generation of founders in their fundraising endeavors for innovative startups.